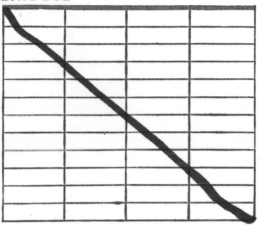

ECONOMICS
and the Truman Administration

ECONOMICS
and the Truman Administration

Edited for
The Harry S. Truman Library Institute
for National and International Affairs
by

Francis H. Heller

THE REGENTS PRESS OF KANSAS
Lawrence

Copyright © 1981 by The Regents Press of Kansas
Printed in the United States of America

Library of Congress Cataloging in Publication Data
Economics and the Truman administration.
"This book has its origin in a conference convened in May 1979 by the Harry
S. Truman Library Institute for National and International Affairs"—Pref.
Bibliography: p.
Includes index.
1. United States—Economic policy—1945-1960—Addresses, essays, lectures.
2. United States. President (1945-1953 : Truman)
I. Heller, Francis Howard.
II. Harry S. Truman Library. Institute for National and International Affairs.
HC106.5.E365   338.973   81-5945
ISBN 0-7006-0217-8   AACR2

Contents

Preface

This book has its origin in a conference convened in May 1979 by the Harry S. Truman Library Institute for National and International Affairs. The purpose was to bring together a number of persons who had played active roles in the making of economic policy during the Truman administration and to place their recollections on record.

The Harry S. Truman Library Institute was formed to lend support to the Truman Library and to promote its interests. The Library itself is, of course, maintained and operated by the National Archives with federal funds. But these funds are not available for the promotion of research and the development of the Library as a major research center. It was President Truman's wish at all times that the library that bears his name and houses his papers should serve scholarly inquiry, and he encouraged the creation of the Institute as a means to channel private support to the advancement of the Library's use by scholars and students. Throughout his life he took an active part in the affairs of the Institute; routinely, he donated to the Institute whatever fees he received for lecturing and speaking engagements. Following his example, a number of his friends and associates have made generous gifts to the Institute, and over five thousand persons, from all walks of life and all parts of the country, contribute annually to the Institute through its Honorary Fellows Program.

Since the Library opened its doors for research in 1959,

the Institute has given over 250 grants to scholars working in the Truman period. In addition, it undertook two special research projects of its own. Every other year the Institute recognizes an outstanding book on the Truman period by the award of a substantial book prize. Its conferences, held on the average of every other year, were initially designed to focus attention on the potential of the Truman period as a research field and of the Truman Library as the major resource center for such research. More recently the conferences have been planned to bring together key officials of the Truman administration to compile something of a collective oral history.

In the present instance, some of the participants had prepared formal statements which, with minor editing, have been incorporated in this volume. Professor Crauford D. Goodwin of Duke University and Robert J. Donovan, author of *Conflict and Crisis: The Presidency of Harry S. Truman, 1945–48* (and a forthcoming sequel covering the years from 1949 to 1953), addressed the conference at its opening session; Professor William J. Barber of Wesleyan University offered a summation at the end. Comments growing out of the discussions have been grouped in two clusters: one focuses on the Employment Act of 1946, the other consists of observations on a range of topics which, while not necessarily related to one another, all relate to the general discussion of economic policy.

The planning of the conference was in the hands of Charles S. Murphy, special counsel to President Truman and now the president of the Truman Library Institute; Dr. Benedict K. Zobrist, director of the Truman Library and secretary of the Institute; and myself. Most of the detail work fell to John Curry of the Truman Library staff to whom I (and all the participants) owe a major debt for his excellent work. Karen Riner typed the manuscript with superior skill and perception. A special word of thanks is due to Professor Darrel Cady of Western Illinois University who, at my request, prepared an exhaustive bibliographical essay that will be invaluable to anyone undertaking research into the economic facets of the Truman administration.

June 1980   Francis H. Heller
Lawrence, Kansas

Contributors

Editor's Note: Only those public positions held during the Truman administration are listed.

William J. Barber, Andrews Professor of Economics, Wesleyan University, author of *A History of Economic Thought* (1967).

Thomas C. Blaisdell, Jr., *Chief of Mission for Economic Affairs, London, 1945–46; Director, Office of International Trade, Department of Commerce, 1947–49; Assistant Secretary of Commerce for International Affairs, 1949–51;* Professor Emeritus of Political Science, University of California, Berkeley.

Charles F. Brannan, *Assistant Secretary of Agriculture, 1944–48; Secretary of Agriculture, 1948–53;* attorney, Denver, Colorado.

Darrel Cady, Associate Professor of History, Western Illinois University.

C. Girard Davidson, *Assistant Secretary of the Interior, 1946–50;* attorney, Portland, Oregon.

Robert J. Donovan, member, Washington Bureau, *New York Herald Tribune,* 1947–63; author of *Conflict and Crisis: The Presidency of Harry S. Truman 1945–48;* Fellow, Woodrow Wilson International Center for Scholars.

Henry H. Fowler, *Deputy Administrator, National Production Authority, Department of Commerce, 1951; Ad-*

ministrator, 1952; Administrator, Defense Production Administration, Director, Offiice of Defense Mobilization, 1952–53; partner, Goldman, Sachs & Co., New York City.

Crauford D. Goodwin, James B. Duke Professor of Economics, Duke University; author and editor of *Exhortation and Controls: The Search for a Wage-Price Policy, 1945–1971* (1975).

Bertram M. Gross, *Executive Secretary, Council of Economic Advisers, 1946–51;* Distinguished Professor of Public Policy and Planning, Hunter College of the City University of New York.

W. Averell Harriman, *Ambassador to the U.S.S.R., 1943–46; Ambassador to the Court of St. James's, 1946; Secretary of Commerce, 1946–48; U.S. Representative in Europe, European Cooperation Administration, 1948–50; Director, Mutual Security Agency, and senior adviser to the President on foreign and military policy, 1951–53.*

Francis H. Heller, Roy A. Roberts Professor of Law and Political Science, University of Kansas; editor of *The Korean War: A 25-Year Perspective* (1977) and *The Truman White House: The Administration of the Presidency, 1945–1953* (1980).

Leon H. Keyserling, *General Counsel, National Housing Agency, 1942–46; member and Vice Chairman, Council of Economic Advisers, 1946–49; Chairman, 1949–53;* President, Conference on Economic Progress, Washington, D.C.

David A. Morse, *Assistant Secretary of Labor, 1945–47; Undersecretary, 1947–48;* attorney, New York City.

Walter S. Salant, *economic adviser to the Economic Stabilization Director, 1945–46; economist, Price Decontrol Board, 1946; staff economist, Council of Economic Advisers, 1946–52;* Senior Fellow Emeritus, Brookings Institution.

John W. Snyder, *Federal Loan Administrator, 1945; Director, Office of War Mobilization and Reconversion, 1945–*

46; Secretary of the Treasury, 1946–53; Chairman, Harry S. Truman Scholarship Foundation.

Frank A. Southard, Jr., *Director, Office of International Finance, Treasury Department, 1947–48; Special Assistant to the Secretary of the Treasury and U.S. Executive Director, International Monetary Fund, 1948–62;* senior associate, Kearns International, Washington, D.C.

Elmer B. Staats, *Chief, War Agencies Section, Bureau of the Budget, 1945–47; Assistant Director, Legislative Reference, 1947–49; Executive Assistant Director, 1949–50; Deputy Director, 1950–53;* Comptroller General of the United States.

David H. Stowe, *Chief Examiner, Bureau of the Budget, 1943–47; Special Assistant to the Assistant to the President, 1947–49; Administrative Assistant to the President, 1949–53;* Chairman, National Mediation Board.

James L. Sundquist, *Administrative analyst, Bureau of the Budget, 1941–47, 1949–51;* Senior Fellow and Director of Governmental Studies, Brookings Institution.

James E. Webb, *Director, Bureau of the Budget, 1946–49; Undersecretary of State, 1949–52;* attorney, Washington, D.C.

Chronology and Statistics

1945

September 2: V-J Day; surrender of Japan ends World War II.

September 6: Truman's 21-point domestic program sent to Congress.

November 21: Strike in the automobile industry.

1946

January 20: Strike in the steel industry.

February 20: Employment Act of 1946 signed into law.

April 1: Strike in the soft-coal industry.

May 18: Nationwide rail strike narrowly averted.

May 21: After 40 days' strike, president seizes coal mines.

June 29: Truman vetoes revised price control bill.

July 25: Truman signs act reviving the Office of Price Administration.

July 29: Edwin G. Nourse appointed first chairman of the Council of Economic Advisers.

October 14: Price controls taken off livestock and meat products.

November 9: All price controls lifted except those on rents, sugar, and rice.

1947

June 23: Labor-Management Relations (Taft-Hartley) Act passed over the president's veto.

November 17: Special session of Congress convenes.

1948

April 2: Tax reduction bill passed over the president's veto.
May 10: Nationwide rail strike averted.
June 30: Fiscal year ends with $8.4 billion surplus, largest ever.

1949

January 5: "Fair Deal" announced in State of the Union message.
April 3: President calls for a Columbia Valley Administration.
October 1: Nationwide steel strike (to November 11).
November 1: Nourse resigns as chairman of the CEA.

1950

April 3: Farm program ("Brannan Plan") sent to Congress.
June 25: North Koreans invade Republic of Korea.
September 8: President given emergency powers under Defense Production Act.

1951

January 26: Most prices and wages frozen.
March 3: Accord between Treasury and Federal Reserve Board.
July 30: Defense Production Act amendments approved.

1952

April 8: Steel industry seized (action held unconstitutional by the Supreme Court, June 2).

STATISTICS

Editor's Note: The following statistics provide an economic profile of the United States during the Truman administration.

Gross National Product, in billions of dollars

FY 1946	FY 1947	FY 1948	FY 1949	FY 1950	FY 1951	FY 1952·
209	231	258	257	285	328	346
−1.5%	10.5%	11.6%	−0.5%	10.9%	15.1%	5.5%

Year-end Consumer Prices (1935–39: 100)

1946	1947	1948	1949	1950	1951	1952
153	167	172	168	177	189	192
19.5%	9.1%	3.0%	−2.4%	5.3%	6.8%	1.6%

Money Supply (demand deposits and currency and net banking system liability), in billions of dollars

FY 1946	FY 1947	FY 1948	FY 1949	FY 1950	FY 1951	FY 1952
118	119	119	119	124	131	137
−11.3%	0.1%	0	0	4.2%	5.6%	4.6%

Federal Reserve Rediscount Rate

FY 1946	FY 1947	FY 1948	FY 1949	FY 1950	FY 1951	FY 1952
1.0%	1.0%	1.5%	1.5%	1.75%	1.75%	1.75%

Ninety-day Treasury Bills, in billions of dollars

FY 1946	FY 1947	FY 1948	FY 1949	FY 1950	FY 1951	FY 1952
0.4	0.6	1.04	1.1	1.22	1.55	1.77

Treasury Surplus or Deficit, in billions of dollars

FY 1946	1947	1948	1949	1950	1951	1952
−19.5	5.7	8.3	−3.0	−1.3	−3.4	−5.8

Year-end Unemployment

1946	1947	1948	1949	1950	1951	1952
....	2.7%	3.3%	5%	3.6%	2.7%	2.7%

Editor's Note: The following statistics reflect the United States payments position and reserves during the Truman administration. (All values are in billions of dollars.)

Gold Reserves

FY 1946	FY 1947	FY 1948	FY 1949	FY 1950	FY 1951	FY 1952
20.5	22.9	25.8	26.0	24.3	24.3	24.7

External Short-term Net Liabilities

FY 1946	FY 1947	FY 1948	FY 1949	FY 1950	FY 1951	FY 1952
5.3	4.3	5.8	6.9	8.9	8.8	10.4

Balance of Payments

FY 1946	FY 1947	FY 1948	FY 1949	FY 1950	FY 1951	FY 1952
7.8	11.3	6.5	5.8	1.8	5.1	5.0

Net use or gain (−) of gold and foreign exchange by foreign countries (includes World Bank and International Monetary Fund net transactions in dollars)

FY 1946	FY 1947	FY 1948	FY 1949	FY 1950	FY 1951	FY 1952
1.9	4.5	1.1	....	−3.6	0.1	−0.8

Government Contribution to the Balance of Payments

FY 1946	FY 1947	FY 1948	FY 1949	FY 1950	FY 1951	FY 1952
5.0	5.7	4.7	5.8	4.0	4.5	4.4

Private Capital Contribution to the Balance of Payments

FY 1946	FY 1947	FY 1948	FY 1949	FY 1950	FY 1951	FY 1952
0.3	0.7	0.9	0.9	1.0	1.2	1.2

1

Introduction

Francis H. Heller

When Harry S. Truman suddenly became president of the United States on April 12, 1945, he inherited not only a world war still to be concluded successfully and the multiplicity of diplomatic problems that would attend the end of the war, he also inherited a broad range of economic questions. The New Deal had stemmed the tide of depression ten years earlier, but the recession of 1938 had raised new fears. Production, first for defense and then for prosecution of the war, had absorbed and enlarged the available labor force. At the same time the demand for agricultural products had sharply increased. The economy boomed. But would it bust again once the wartime stimulation was gone? Sharp divisions of opinion existed as to how the reconversion to a peacetime economy should be handled. There were prophets of gloom who predicted that a major recession, perhaps a full-fledged depression, could not be avoided once the fighting ended.

Harry Truman was no economist, but neither was he unfamiliar with the challenge of economic issues. The populism of midwestern farm life was a major force in his background. He had learned the hard way in his early ventures into business, both before and after World War I, how difficult it is for the small entrepreneur to succeed. As Jackson County (Missouri) administrator he had dealt with the many factors, both political and economic, that buffet the public sector. In the United States Senate he had, rather more than other senators, been involved with matters of an economic nature. As far as is known, he had not read economic theories—indeed, he was generally leery of theorists and theoretical talk—but he had studied and he understood their practical manifestations.

As a senator, Truman had been a loyal and consistent supporter of the New Deal. Upon his succession to the presidency, he committed himself to a continuation of the Roosevelt policies. One may safely assume—especially in light of F.D.R.'s failure to share his foreign policy concerns with his vice-president—that Truman was thinking of the New Deal. His first major message to the Congress, in September 1945, of course, bears all the hallmarks of the New Deal.

Out of his own experiences Harry Truman carried a strong conviction that the nation's welfare was closely tied to the fortunes of the "little man"—the independent farmer, the small businessman, the workingman. If inflation hit, these were the individuals who would suffer the most. If the government's obligations (bonds) lost in value, these people would be the ones who would find it hardest to absorb the loss. Truman's ideas on monetary policies— strongly shared and supported by his good friend and long-time secretary of the treasury, John W. Snyder—always placed a high value on keeping the dollar sound and the government's credit stable.

The idea of economic growth was the link, both in theory and practice, between the New Deal's (and Fair Deal's) commitment to public expenditures for the social good and the president's firm belief in a balanced budget and sound money. Under the articulate leadership of Leon H. Keyserling, the president's Council of Economic Advisers (itself an innovation of the Truman years) consistently proclaimed its faith in the ability of the American economy to face any challenge as long as it was allowed to grow as its dynamics would make it.

It is probably important to keep in mind (as James Sundquist points out in these pages) that it was not until 1946 that a president of the United States was required by law to enunciate an economic policy. The Employment Act of 1946, which established this requirement, is thus a truly fundamental piece of legislation, an act that materially affects the nature of our government. Keyserling, Bertram Gross, Walter Salant, and Sundquist provide various insights into the genesis of this law and assess its impact. At times in their discussion there surfaces the question (which is also touched on in Crauford Goodwin's opening essay) of the influence of John Maynard Keynes. William Barber in his summation opines parenthetically that future scholars may not become "overly exercised" about this issue, but in 1979 it still evoked discussion.

Understandably, the contributors to this volume dwell at some length on the achievements and successes of the Truman administration. Of course, the road was rocky, and kibitzers, then and later, did not hold back on criticism. This volume does not purport to be a definitive historical treatment. As Darrel Cady's bibliographical essay indicates, a great deal of work remains to be done before any claim to historical completeness can be made. Surely, however, the record would be incomplete without the views and the recollections contributed here.

2

The Economic Problems
Facing Truman

Crauford A. Goodwin

In the spring of 1945, President Truman faced two kinds of economic challenges: first, those that he and most of his associates recognized quite well at the time; and second, those that only today we see were emerging then and which would grow to plague Americans for years to come.

Without doubt, the single economic problem most prominently on people's minds in 1945 was how to reconvert the economy from a wartime to a peacetime basis. All the instruments of mobilization had been developed by President Roosevelt, and at the time of his death it seemed clear that they would be adequate to finish the wartime job without substantial modification. What made the task of reconversion so frightening was the possibility, and even the likelihood, that peace would bring a return to serious depression. Three aspects of the 1930s depression were especially worrisome: first, the unemployment and personal hardship it created; second, the stagnation in the growth of national production which some feared might foretell a long-term trend; and third, the differential rates of suffering among regions (for example, the South) and among occupational groups (like the farmers of the Southwest).

A variety of factors complicated reconversion. Perhaps the most important was the difficulty in obtaining a persuasive diagnosis of which problems were liable to emerge in peacetime. Not only were politicians and bureaucrats divided along party and ideological lines over these questions, but professional economists were also either split or ambivalent.

One position was that the depression had as its source structural weaknesses in the American economic system. Therefore, a fundamental reform of institutions, ranging from agricultural markets to collective bargaining, was needed to assure the maintenance of adequate purchasing power and equitable distribution. This view was associated, in particular, with "institutionalist" economists and had deep roots in the New Deal.

A second approach was to say that, indeed, economic depression grew out of inadequate effective demand, but that the solution might lie simply in the manipulation of the tools of fiscal and monetary policy. Both of these approaches prescribed substantial government intervention in the economy as preventive medicine; but the second (which is, of course, associated mainly with John Maynard Keynes, even though it had some indigenous American roots as well) was far less radical and less threatening to established interests. This distinction was recognized quite early by such business groups as the Committee for Economic Development in its support of Keynesian policy.

Still a third approach urged government to intervene in the economy as little as possible, lest by its actions it worsen the very problems it was attempting to solve. In 1945 such libertarians as Henry Simons of the University of Chicago were warning Americans that the very survival of the free-market system was threatened by the proposals for postwar policy advanced by the institutionalists and the Keynesians. So when President Truman—faced with economic advice that recommended "on the one hand and on the other"—made his celebrated and probably apocryphal appeal for a one-armed economist, he might have wished alternatively for fewer pairs of arms from which to choose.

Overriding all worries about how to cope with reconversion was the prevailing desire to get on with it. In part, this was merely a natural response from people who, accustomed to economic freedom, had been cribbed and cabined for four years. And in part, it reflected a widespread belief among groups in many parts of the economy that they, in particular, stood to gain from an end to controls.

Thus, a central question regarding reconversion was how to deal with the pent-up demand for consumer goods and services which everyone agreed had accumulated during the war. The fear was that if this demand were released suddenly, prices would skyrocket and bring on a collapse. Consumer groups, in particular, urged the government to keep controls in place until 1947 or 1948 so that the resources diverted to war could be redirected to produce consumer goods and sufficient productivity could be generated to absorb the increased effective demand—at constant prices. On the other hand, most business spokesmen thought that if government expenditures were reduced drastically and quickly, controls could be removed much earlier without danger of inflation. On this question, the experience of post–World War I reconversion was cited more often than any sophisticated economic analysis.

Against the background of how to accomplish reconversion smoothly, the special problems and fears of particular segments of the economy had to be faced. The farmers, who had operated through a range of wartime institutions and other New Deal devices designed to stabilize both their prices and their incomes, remained nervous and suspicious that, while peace might bring plenty to the nation, for them it could mean a return to poverty. Farmers worried that the buoyant markets of the war years were the result of unusual circumstances—in particular, of the beneficial effects of price controls for consumers. As one congressman remarked to Price Administrator Chester Bowles in a congressional hearing in June 1945: "The thing I am wondering is how the housewife who has been paying ten cents for a loaf of bread is going to react when eleven-cent bread comes in after this is over."

Under the National Labor Relations Act, trade unions had been given a bill of rights. But neither they, employers, nor society itself had yet seen how the new system of collective bargaining would operate without the discipline of substantial unemployment or war. With the onset of much labor strife as the war ended, auguries were not good.

After the abortive experiment of the National Recovery Administration [NRA] and the spotlight of negative publicity from the Temporary National Economic Committee, corporations had enjoyed a measure of "partnership" with government during the war. Questions of antitrust activity and market concentration were temporarily put in abeyance or at least muted. But it was obvious to everyone that these issues would quickly surface again when peace and prosperity returned. A particular problem for President Truman—and for business—was to decide just what role industry and other special interests should assume at the end of war. The various industry councils and committees had played an indispensable part during the emergency. Could they now be converted to a useful peacetime role?

A crucial question that had plagued President Roosevelt during much of the last years of his life was America's proper posture in the postwar world. President Truman inherited this question, with only parts of the answer well formulated and very little personal experience to go on. Many aspects of the question were economic. For example, what system of world currency and finance could be erected to replace the gold standard which had broken down during the 1930s? What new arrangements could be made to perform the useful and important economic functions of the various European empires? How could access to materials and export markets be assured to reduce the possibility of a future war for *Lebensraum*? Most commentators agreed that America would have to take the lead in organizing the world trading system. Today it is poignant to read that their main concern was to try to decide what goods the United States could possibly want to purchase from the rest of the world!

The challenge for the Truman administration was not only to devise economic policies appropriate for peacetime at home and abroad, but also to construct the governmental institutions that would make these policies work. President Truman was heir to a number of highly creative institutional initiatives that were just coming to fruition as he took office. Internationally, these were the Bretton Woods negotiations, the International Bank for Reconstruction and Development [IBRD], and the International Monetary Fund [IMF]. On the home front, hearings on the full employment bill were held in 1945 and yielded the idea for a Council of Economics Advisers [CEA] and the Joint Economic Committee, both of which came into existence a year later.

But a great deal more had to be done in creating new mechanisms. World-wide, there was a clear danger that nations would slip back into commercial autarky; international institutions were needed to promote free trade. Moreover, the way to accomplish bilateral assistance from rich countries to poor countries was still unknown. (It would reach a high point of achievement, however, in a remarkably short time under President Truman in the form of the European Recovery Program and Point Four.) Throughout the federal government the challenge was to introduce economic knowledge and skills into the formulation of coherent policy. Economics was needed beyond, simply, the new CEA, the Treasury, and the Budget Bureau (where traditionally economic wisdom was thought to lie). The times cried out for improved economic skills in Interior, Labor, Commerce, Agriculture, and, of course, in the State Department with its new international responsibilities. Nor was it only the executive branch that needed a better grasp of economics. Congress, the press, and the public were often both confused and fearful about matters economic. Moreover, the general suspicion often extended to economists themselves. It was not only that they practiced black arts, it was also that they seemed somehow to be identified with planning, socialism, and—so it was said—even the dreaded totalitarianism of the Axis powers.

With memories of the depression still fresh, it was hard to persuade the public of the allocative efficiency of free markets—the economists' stock in trade. In fact, in some markets any price change had come to be viewed as evidence of a conspiratorial manipulation by either sellers or buyers, depending on whether prices were going up or down. At the macro-economic level, deficits in the federal budget were still widely perceived as the result of moral turpitude; and increases in interest rates were seen as a device to defraud bondholders of their property. Such old chestnuts as the "lump-of-labor fallacy" were often voiced: for example, the head of a major union in July 1945 called for a reduction in the work week to thirty-five hours so as to share the available jobs. In such an environment even the most omniscient policymaker was constrained by his constituency.

It is worth emphasizing the state of disarray that existed in the economics profession in 1945. Above all, the catastrophe of the depression made people doubt whether economists really knew what they were talking about. Macro-economics was just emerging, somewhat uncertainly. In micro-economics, New Deal policies and the success of war-time regulation made the free market seem almost an anachronism. With the apparent decline of the free market, and thus of this means to assure both economic equity and efficiency, the fundamental question of a replacement was raised. There were three schools of thought on how to organize an alternative system.

1. *Restore competition.* Advocates of this position were found chiefly in the Anti-Trust Division of the Justice Department and among libertarian economists.

2. *Plan,* i.e., create bureaucratic institutions to replace the free market. The roots of this idea go back well into the 1920s and 1930s, but it was given a powerful boost by the war and by successful devices like the Office of Price Administration [OPA] and even the Board of Economic Warfare [BEW].

3. *Find some middle ground* between laissez faire and central planning, such as the economist J. M. Clark's "workable competition."

When one reads the newspapers, magazines, and public addresses of the months surrounding President Truman's accession to office, it is striking how many of the problems that are high on the nation's agenda today were more or less clearly perceived as problems then. To begin with, inflation was seen by many as a serious threat—granted, it was viewed mainly as a one-time explosion after the end of price controls or only as a prelude to recession, but inflation was on their minds all the same. Within the Interior Department, at least, the long-term supply of energy and natural resources was causing concern. America's independence in this regard was seen as slipping away. The rapid rural-urban migration, especially from the South to northern cities, was recognized as a likely source of social, economic, and political friction in the future. It is even striking to find the author Louis Bromfield, in an address to the Executive Club of Chicago in March 1945, making a plea for the environment in a fashion that would have pleased Barry Commoner thirty years later. Persons as varied as Prof. Harley L. Lutz of Princeton, a liberal, and Hugh Butler, the conservative senator from Nebraska, attracted attention by appealing for a ceiling on the federal debt and for balanced budgets. Although they did not call for a constitutional convention, they were moving in that direction. And in 1945 a physicians' forum endorsed the idea of compulsory national health insurance. This was a yeasty time indeed.

Thus, President Truman came to office with an extraordinarily wide array of economic problems facing him. The central question was how best to reconvert from war to peace, and in fact, this dilemma was to consume his early months in office. But other problems were certainly as challenging and often more intractable. Still, the mood was optimistic both in private industry and among economists and policymakers. This helps explain why the years from 1946 to 1950 were a golden age of creative economic policymaking in America.

I have searched, unsystematically, for periods in history which may be comparable to the Truman years with respect to the formation of economic policy. The years immediately after the Napoleonic Wars in Britain seem to be the only good candidate—for several reasons. First, both periods witnessed major debate among politicians and economists about the broad economic questions growing out of reconversion from war and fear of depression. Then, the issues were whether to increase free trade, whether to deflate the currency to restore the old parity, and whether to encourage emigration or deal with population growth in other ways. Second, in both periods a dominant economic theorist of a few years before loomed large, and much of the debate centered on whether to implement the conclusion of his model. For post-Napoleonic Britain, it was Adam Smith and free markets; for post–World War II America, it was John Maynard Keynes and the manipulation of the economy to achieve full employment. Third, in both periods new professionals emerged (Ricardo, Mill, Malthus then—Samuelson, Friedman, Galbraith later), and relatively spectacular results were manifest in due course. In post-Napoleonic Britain, it was repeal of the Corn Laws and Navigation Acts; in post–World War II America, it was the tax cut of 1964. Finally, these combinations of circumstances in both periods led to big thinking on broad systemic issues, such as the world economic system (Britain's relations to its colonies and later the Bretton Woods conference), and to an improvement in human welfare. One only wishes that there had been a conference thirty-five years after the Battle of Waterloo wherein the policymakers of that postwar period could review their experiences and achievements.

3

Truman's Perspective

Robert J. Donovan

President Truman probably would not have favored Proposition 13*: it would have struck him as a gimmick. On the other hand, all the devoutness, the fervor, we see now about a balanced budget reminds us of Mr. Truman's predilection for not spending more money than the government took in.

In the heady 1960s, Truman's fiscal principles made him seem old-fashioned. Now, in the hard times of 1979, he appears as modern as Gov. Jerry Brown of California. Indeed, one can almost imagine President Carter and Secretary of the Treasury [Michael] Blumenthal talking the way Mr. Truman and John Snyder used to, planning to accumulate a surplus in good years to pay off some of the national debt.

Whatever else Mr. Truman knew about modern economic theory, he certainly understood that deficit spending contributes to inflation. Curiously, however, as a new reporter in Washington in 1947, one of my earliest experiences was listening to the elemental voice of John Tabor of New York, the Republican chairman of the House Appropriations Committee, condemning the wild spending policies of the Truman administration. Speaker Joe Martin said something to the effect that we must "re-man the citadel of

---

* An initiative proposal adopted by the voters of California in 1978 to reduce property taxes. Its adoption triggered widespread agitation for tax reduction and levy limits. [Ed.]

liberty." It took a while for this newcomer to see the whole picture.

President Truman was a man of moderate economic policies on the whole, a middle-of-the-roader, as most of our presidents are; after all, the center is where most of the votes are. In a practical way, over a long lifetime, Mr. Truman had learned first hand a good deal about the economics of the farm and of a small business. As the chief administrator of Jackson County, Missouri, he came to grips with the economics of local government. Later he got a close look at the workings of corporations and labor unions as chairman of the Senate Special Committee to Investigate the National Defense Program (the Truman Committee, as it was called). And his years on the Senate Appropriations Committee gave him a grounding in the complexities of the federal budget.

I remember after he suddenly became president how astounded the press was at his working knowledge of the budget. To be sure, understanding local and federal budgets is not the same as having a grasp of, and being able to analyze, national and international economic problems. But as a breed, presidents are not economists; we have never had a professional economist in the White House. Mr. Truman was a pragmatist, not a theorist. What he brought to economic problems was experience in governmental affairs and common sense.

Without attempting to adjudicate these points, let me cite two views about his handling of economic problems. (The views are not necessarily mutually exclusive.) The first grew out of a heated conflict in 1950 and 1951 between the Treasury and the Federal Reserve Board. The issue was the continuance of a wartime commitment by the Federal Reserve to support the price of government securities at predetermined levels. Many will recall Mr. Truman's repeated allusions to his own experiences as a soldier in the First World War. He had bought government bonds at the rate of $100 and then, when he needed the money upon his return to civilian life, was able to sell them at a rate of only $82. The experience seemed to have had a strong influence on him throughout his life. He believed that if a citizen paid $100 for a government bond, he should be able to sell it for no less than $100. That was typical of Mr. Truman's feelings of propriety and his common sense about things, including economics.

He was, therefore, quite taken aback when in 1950 and 1951 the Federal Reserve began sliding away from its commitment to support government securities, causing a sag in long-term bonds. The president insisted that the Federal Reserve stand by its commitment and maintain the price. The view from the Federal Reserve was that while Mr. Truman's position was a decent one, it was simplistic. Officials at the Federal Reserve Board held that the law of supply and demand—in other words, market forces—governed the pattern of the bond market. By this reasoning, the Federal Reserve could not have held interest rates at a certain level without taking measures that would have caused severe inflation. Yet Federal Reserve officials were dismayed to find that the question of market forces played little part in Mr. Truman's thinking on this problem.

His common-sense view was that the right thing was for the price of government bonds to be kept stable and that it was the duty of the Federal Reserve to insure this. Mr. Truman, incidentally, did not prevail. To the end of his term, I suspect he felt that the Federal Reserve was not doing its duty.

The Truman years were, by the way, a rough period for the chairmen of the Federal Reserve Board. In 1948 Mr. Truman had refused to reappoint Marriner Eccles when his term as chairman expired. Among other reasons, Mr. Truman was said to feel that the Federal Reserve was becoming too powerful; he himself said he wanted to show Eccles who was boss. Mr. Truman replaced Eccles with Thomas McCabe, but then forced his resignation in 1951 in the dispute over the price of bonds.

The president's next chairman was William McChesney Martin, Jr., who remained in that post for the rest of of the Truman administration—and indeed until 1970. But

Mr. Truman seems not to have been much more satisfied with Mr. Martin than with his predecessors, because he did not hold the line on bond prices. Mr. Martin evidently doubted that it ever could have been held and, I gather, declined to give any kind of assurance when the president appointed him.

For another view, I refer to Professor Goodwin's valuable book *Exhortation and Controls: The Search for a Wage-Price Policy, 1945–1971* (1975). Professor Goodwin takes the position that the Truman administration's approach to economics was not simplistic. To this might be added the observation that no one who has watched the handiwork of subsequent administrations, including the current one, is likely to be impressed with the results of any new, sophisticated economics emerging at 1600 Pennsylvania Avenue. Professor Goodwin makes the point that virtually all the causes of inflation, as they are understood today, were discussed during the Truman administration. And he notes: "Almost a whole armory of weapons against inflation was also reviewed and tried, monetary restraints, budget surpluses, jaw boning of businessmen, unions and consumers, partial controls, full controls, guideposts, freezes . . . and direct intervention in the operation of key industries." Professor Goodwin concludes: "Advances were made in the politics as well as in the economics of inflation under Truman."

I would like to examine in some detail the administration's direct intervention in the operation of key industries, as a device to combat inflation. This was one of Mr. Truman's most unusual economic initiatives, originally suggested by Assistant Secretary of the Interior C. Girard Davidson and pressed by Walter P. Reuther, president of the United Automobile Workers.

In his 1949 State of the Union message, President Truman requested authority for the federal government to build steel plants or other facilities if private industry, on its own, failed to meet the country's need for basic products. The administration had been concerned about the effect of restricted production in forcing up prices in a few critical industries—particularly steel. Because that industry consisted of so few sellers, some government economists believed that it simply did not respond to market forces. During good times, they said, the industry failed to increase capacity in response to demand, either because the steel companies benefited from limited production or because they feared a future recession. Hence, steel prices rose and ultimately restrained activity elsewhere in the economy.

Mr. Truman's proposal caused quite a stir and never did get through Congress. He later disclaimed any intention of putting the government in the steel business and likened the plan to that of the wartime Defense Plants Corporation which, he said, built $20 million worth of plants, most of which were integrated with private plants.

During the Truman administration, economic policy passed through three distinct phases. The first, an utterly hectic time, was the period immediately following the Second World War. I remember from personal experiences that it was a time of tremendous contention. Labor and business, consumer and farmer, all were at each other's throats. It was a time when Republicans saw a chance, at last, to kill the New Deal, and it was a time when we had the greatest wave of labor unrest and strikes in American history. Postwar policy was hammered out in a welter of emotion and conflict and jockeying for political position.

My own recollection is that, for all this, we got through the postwar period remarkably speedily and remarkably well. There was inflation—and those of us who were around then felt it—but we never had inflation as rampant as today.

Hard on the heels of reconversion was the period when economic policy became interwoven with Cold War diplomacy. The centerpiece of this period was, of course, the Marshall Plan. This multibillion dollar program had various purposes; from the outset it was recognized that one of them was to stimulate trade and thus ensure jobs and prosperity in America—and it did just that.

During those same years, 1947 through 1949, there

occurred within the administration a deep conflict about military spending that provides some fascinating glimpses into the way President Truman's mind worked on economic questions.

To simplify, after the Second World War, America drastically demobilized its armed forces. Then the nation found itself at odds with the Soviet Union: the Cold War was on; trouble boiled up in Iran; the Communists seized Czechoslovakia; Berlin was blockaded. In the face of these new dangers and responsibilities, Secretary of Defense [James V.] Forrestal and the Joint Chiefs of Staff recommended a major increase in the armed forces to bring our military power into balance with our international obligations.

In view of unforeseen challenges ahead, notably in Korea, this was to be a decision of great importance. Other elements entered into Mr. Truman's judgment, of course, but the economic ones were uppermost. While allowing a moderate increase in military spending, he not only rejected a major expansion but also imposed rigid ceilings on military budgets. The Pentagon's request for new appropriations simply ran up against Mr. Truman's desire for a balanced budget.

In 1948, over his veto, the Republican-controlled Eightieth Congress cut taxes. Because of the resulting loss of revenue and because of the continuing cost of the Marshall Plan, the prospect was for a budget deficit, which disturbed Mr. Truman. He had a great deal of respect for the views of his conservative fiscal advisers, who generally favored holding down military spending. In fact, in reading the record, one gets the impression that he was more attentive to the advice of his fiscal advisers than he was to the strategic concerns of the military leaders. In 1948 and 1949, the consensus in Washington was that it would be ruinously expensive to spend more than $15 billion annually on defense. This was, as Charles Murphy, then special counsel to the president, has remarked, conventional wisdom in the White House as well. Referring to the $15 billion figure in 1948, Mr. Truman said, "We can't keep that up."

This consensus was reinforced by another: that the Soviet Union was deliberately trying to scare the United States into spending itself into bankruptcy. The president worried that, once a major military expansion had been authorized, military spending would inevitably escalate and would be impossible to stop year after year. Thus, Mr. Truman stood firm, a decision he himself later came to doubt. "He is a hard-money man if I ever saw one," said Forrestal, who understood the president rather better than Congressman Taber did.

Finally, the Korean War (particularly the Chinese intervention in the fighting) marked the last phase of economic policy under Mr. Truman. Unfortunately, the Korean War sidetracked a number of programs that might otherwise have come to fruition in the latter part of the Truman administration. The danger of wartime inflation drove the administration to impose an array of economic controls—wage and price controls among them—on the pattern of those instituted during the Second World War. Fear that Communist actions in Korea might precede aggression in Europe or the Middle East led to a huge increase in military spending along the lines visualized in NSC-68, the comprehensive concept for our defense policy adopted by the National Security Council shortly before the outbreak of the Korean War.

This spending marked an historic turning point. It made possible a great expansion of the American military establishment. It financed the rearmament of Allied countries, particularly those in the North Atlantic Treaty Organization [NATO]. It also marked the end, for all time, of $15 billion defense budgets. And it set the country on the road to years of heavy military spending with profound effects, even now, on the political, economic, and social life of the country and on national priorities in general.

Mr. Truman faced up to the economic dilemma of war better than some other presidents have. Believing that Franklin Roosevelt had financed too much of the Second World War off-the-cuff, Mr. Truman, at Secretary Snyder's urging, got a series of major tax bills through Congress to pay for the fighting (something that was badly lacking later in the Vietnam War).

The story of economic controls during the Korean War is a long and complex one. It was a nasty time for President Truman: the trauma of limited war compounded the task of leadership. Economic controls were unpopular and difficult to administer even during the Second World War, when people generally believed in fighting an all-out war against Nazi Germany and Japan. The frustrations of the limited war in Korea absolutely soured the national mood and immersed the management of controls in boisterous contention and partisan clash, which was heightened by the approaching 1952 presidential elections. Out of the turmoil came Mr. Truman's decision to seize control of the steel industry, a question on which he accepted some particularly bad advice.

Looking back at the history of economic policy during the years from 1945 through 1952, one is struck by the tough role destiny handed Mr. Truman. He had barely become president when he had to shoulder the monstrous task of guiding the country through postwar reconversion. And then in his final period in office he had to engage in months of tumultuous struggle to keep the economy going through the Korean War. It was not a time for tidy policies; the road was rough all the way.

Like all presidents, Mr. Truman had his failures and his successes. But he knew what he wanted and perhaps best expressed it in a letter written after the 1948 election to Charles E. Wilson, the head of General Electric:

> I am sure that right down in your heart you know that the ordinary man is the backbone of any country, particularly is that true in a republic, and what I am trying to do is eliminate the fringe at each end of the situation. I think small business, the small farmer, the small corporations, are the backbone of any free society, and when there are too many people on relief and too many peo-

ple at the top who control the wealth of this country, then we must look out.

He concluded: "I expect to give everybody, big and little, a fair deal and nothing less."

4

The Treasury
And Economic Policy

John W. Snyder

The seven and a half years following the close of World War II were a time of important developments in fiscal policies and operations. In this essay I will review the functioning of the nation's finances during this period, which coincides with my terms of office as director of the Office of War Mobilization and Reconversion [OWMR] and as secretary of the treasury.

During the Truman administration, the government had to adjust first to the problems arising from the aftermath of the war and subsequently to the task of rearming to meet the Communist challenge. Accordingly, I shall describe the major measures taken to finance the government's activities and will outline the whole range of Treasury policies—including debt management, taxation, international financial relations, and improvements in operating activities—against the background of national economic developments.

One of the major problems facing the Treasury when I took the oath of office on June 25, 1946, was how to achieve a balance between revenues and expenditures that would produce a surplus which could then be used to reduce the national debt. When I took office, I said: "It is the responsibility of the government to reduce its expenditures in every possible way, to maintain adequate tax rates . . . and to achieve a balanced budget . . . or better. . . ."

The problems involved in changing from a deficit situation to a balanced budget—or better—were extremely complex. There was widespread public agitation for an across-the-board reduction in taxes and for the abolition of various special taxes which had been instituted during the war. While many improvements in the structure of our wartime tax system were clearly called for, the enormity of our wartime spending made it imperative that we also reduce the national debt. By the middle of 1946, it was clear that these would be tasks of major proportions. Our public debt had increased five-fold during World War II and amounted to $270 billion on June 30, 1946. This figure represented 60 percent of all outstanding debt, public and private, as compared with the government's share of less than 25 percent in 1939, before we began our World War II defense and war-financing programs.

It is possible to divide the economic events of the Truman administration into four periods: reconversion and inflation, 1945–48; recession and recovery, 1949–50; the Korean War, 1950–51; and the final period, 1952–53.

Reconversion and Inflation, 1945–48

In 1945, at the end of the war, the United States had a full-employment, war-mobilized economy governed by price and wage controls and rationing. The task confronting the government was to decontrol and demobilize the economy without falling prey to the sharp boom-and-collapse cycle which had followed World War I.

In his special message (delivered September 6, 1945, and prepared largely by my OWMR staff) President Truman presented a reconversion program that included five main points.

1. Provide for unemployment compensation and increase the minimum wage (then only forty cents).

2. Gradually decontrol prices and wage rates and eliminate rationing and allocations.

3. Make full employment a policy goal. (This resulted in the Employment Act of 1946, which established the Council of Economic Advisers and the Joint Economic Committee of Congress, both of which continue today—the former after

a brief hiatus in the early months of the Eisenhower administration.)

4. Recast agricultural policy, strengthening price supports and providing crop insurance.

5. Enact comprehensive housing legislation to support construction of 1.0 to 1.5 million units per year.

Speaking broadly, this program was carried out. The Gross National Product [GNP], after declining 1.5 percent in 1946 (reflecting end-of-war dislocations) increased 10.5 percent in 1947. The task of absorbing the demobilized labor force was handled remarkably smoothly. In mid 1947, unemployment was about 4 percent; by year-end it had declined to 2.7 percent.

We had less success in the area of prices and inflation. From the end of hostilities to mid 1946, consumer prices had risen 3 percent and wholesale prices, 7.9 percent. But between July and December 1946, following the removal of price controls, consumer prices rose at an annual rate of 30 percent and wholesale prices increased 50 percent—the highest rate ever. This trend continued, although at a less hectic rate. After leveling off in the first half of 1947, consumer prices rose 12 percent and wholesale prices were up 20 percent (annual rates) in the second half. By the end of 1947, consumer prices were 9.1 percent above the December 1946 mark. This jump was, perhaps, unavoidable: consumer savings were high; pent-up demand was released; consumer credit was liberal; and construction was booming.

The government's policy was aimed at countering inflation. After a deficit of $19 billion in 1946, there was a surplus of $5.7 billion in 1947; tax reduction, however, was ruled out as an anti-inflationary measure. Monetary policy, on the other hand, was passive. Federal Reserve support of the government bond market continued until early 1950, and interest and discount rates remained very low.

President Truman declared that the first objective for 1948 must be to halt the inflationary trend. On November 17, 1947, he outlined a ten-point program. Its main elements were: (1) restraints on credit and speculation; (2) allocation of scarce commodities; (3) strengthening of rent control; (4) authority to impose selective rationing and price control; (5) budgeting for a fiscal surplus; and (6) strengthening the credit-control powers of the Federal Reserve System.

By the end of 1948, the economic and financial picture showed the results of the government's policies of restraint and of the ebbing of postwar buying and speculation. In August, prices reached a peak of 4.5 percent over December 1947 and then declined by year-end to 3 percent. By any standard, this was a remarkable stabilization. At the same time, the GNP increased 11.1 percent, and unemployment ranged from 3 to 3.3 percent. The budget surplus was $8.3 million—actually, in the first half of 1948 the cash surplus was $12 billion—and this was a major counter-inflationary factor. Monetary policy was as firm as the Fed's continuing support of the bond market allowed: reserve requirements were raised, and there was a small increase in the discount rate. The money supply did not increase.

From the close of World War II, the Treasury Department and the Federal Reserve System were agreed upon a fundamental goal: to maintain a high level of production, employment, and income with as much price stability as possible under the cyclical conditions of a dynamic economy. The agencies were also in agreement on several other objectives: (1) maintaining confidence in the government's credit; (2) maintaining a sound market for the government's securities; (3) restraining, during much of the period, overall credit expansion; (4) increasing the ownership of government securities by nonbank investors and reducing the holdings of the banking system; and (5) adjusting the wartime pattern of interest rates from time to time, as it became appropriate.

There were occasional differences of opinion over which techniques should be used to reach these objectives. But there was never any disagreement as to the fundamental goal: to promote stable economic growth through sound credit and debt policy while meeting the fiscal requirements of the government. In fact, the Treasury and the Federal Reserve worked closely together on several programs. For example, they cooperated in a debt-reduction program that concentrated on the holdings of commercial banks. Both agencies encouraged savings throughout the economy. And they agreed that selective credit controls and other selective restraints should be used to control inflationary pressures.

During the war, it had not been possible to modernize operations in the Treasury Department on the basis of new technology and procedures; recruitment of competent personnel, likewise, was severely restricted. Consequently, the tremendous wartime increase in Treasury operations had to be handled by the restricted facilities of a department geared to a low, prewar volume of operations.

In 1946, although the war was over, a great part of the expanded volume of Treasury operations nevertheless remained. There was an urgent need to modernize and streamline the department's services so that it could meet the increased responsibilities of the federal government. In response to these needs, I began several modernization and reorganization programs, including the reorganization and improvement in management of the Bureau of Internal Revenue; improvement in the services and operation procedures of the United States Coast Guard; improvement in the overall accounting and financial procedures of the federal government; and increased efficiency in the Treasury Department's working operations and in its service to the public. This last program was accomplished with the help of management-efficiency studies within the department, management surveys by private management-engineering firms, and the participation of all departmental employees (through a system of cash awards for efficiency, superior accomplishments, and management-improvement suggestions).

Recession and Recovery, 1949–50

The president was cautious in making his policy and legislative proposals in January 1949—which was a prudent move since the stability of prices was both newly won and fragile. He emphasized the need for a continuing budget surplus and requested an extension of the Federal Reserve powers—which were due to expire July 1—to require supplementary reserves and to regulate consumer credit. He also requested and won the powers to order allocation of key materials, to institute selective price and wage controls, and to extend rent control for two years.

Despite these efforts, 1949 saw the first recession of the postwar period. The GNP scarcely increased; consumer prices actually declined 2.4 percent; and by the end of the year, unemployment had reached 5 percent. During the early part of the year there had been a fiscal surplus and a further retirement of public debt. But, as the normal consequence of recession, in addition to the effects of the 1948 tax reduction and increases in defense expenditures, there was a fiscal deficit of $3 billion for the year as a whole. This fiscal posture continued during the first half of 1950, with a deficit of $4.3 billion. The Federal Reserve moved to ease credit. On March 4, 1950, the Treasury-Federal Reserve accord, which had been worked out between the two agencies, became effective and freed credit policy from the need to support the government securities market.

During the first half of 1950, the economy clearly was emerging from the recession. The president's program, announced in January, reflected this improving state of affairs. He stressed the need to maintain steady economic growth, setting a target for the GNP of $300 billion within five years, up from the 1949 level of $257 billion. (In fact, the 1954 GNP was $363 billion.) Unemployment, the president said, should be reduced from 3.5 million to 2.5 million, and the tax structure must provide a better income distribution. In addition, productivity must be increased; fiscal policy must contribute to growth, with a balanced budget over a period of years and a budget surplus in good years. Finally, Mr. Truman proposed that there should be sound social programs, with attention to low-income groups and depressed areas. But the situation was to change drastically in June with the onset of the Korean War.

The Korean War, 1950–51

The invasion of Korea set off a new economic disturbance throughout the world. Prices rose, and increased military spending added to the generally inflationary pressures in many countries. Large imports by the United States resulted in considerable additions to the gold and dollar reserves of the sterling area and other raw-material producing countries; but the high price of raw materials adversely affected European manufacturing centers.

The outbreak of hostilities on June 25, followed by the entrance of Chinese troops in November, totally changed both the economic developments in this country and the administration's policies and actions. The country was rapidly back on a war footing. Between June 15 and July 15, a wave of buying pushed the Consumer Price Index [CPI] up 1.4 percent in 30 days; by the end of 1950 the index was up 5 percent over 1949. Raw materials and construction supplies were in demand and inventories rose. By the end of the year, industrial prices were rising; unemployment fell to 3.6 percent; and the GNP had increased by 10.9 percent over 1949.

Fiscal policy was promptly adjusted to meet the new situation. In July the president requested, and Congress granted, tax increases of about $5 billion, and in November the president recommended an "excess profits" tax. The fiscal result was a deficit of only $1.3 billion, thanks to a surplus during the first half of the year. The Federal Reserve tightened consumer and housing credit. On December 16 a state of national emergency was declared; the Office of Defense Mobilization was established; and the Economic Stabilization Agency was empowered to institute price and wage controls.

In his Economic Report to Congress in January 1951, President Truman cited the huge increase in defense expenditures from $18 billion in fiscal 1950 to a likely annual rate of $45 to $55 billion by the end of 1951. (This figure would be 18 percent of the GNP as against 45 percent at the peak of World War II.) Thus, administration policies were to be aimed at expanding production (the Defense Production Act of September 1950), training manpower, improving health services, stabilizing prices and wages, and increasing both taxes and restraints on credit.

Truman's fiscal policy was designed to pay the entire cost of the defense program with tax rates substantially higher than at the peak of World War II. The administration's credit policy was aimed at achieving a smooth transition to defense mobilization, assisting debt management, and minimizing inflation. Selective credit controls would be needed.

The results of the 1951 budget were very good, considering the surge of public expenditures. A surplus of $4.1 billion was generated in the first half of the year, followed by a deficit of $7.5 billion in the second. Thus, the total deficit for the year was $3.4 billion. Consumer prices rose 8 percent between the outbreak of war in June 1950 and the price freeze in February 1951; from that point to the end of the year, they rose less than 3 percent. The increase for the year was 6.8 percent. And by the end of 1951, unemployment decreased to 2.7 percent.

The Final Period, 1952–53

After the recession of 1949 and the impact of the Korean War, the last year of the Truman administration was a vast economic and financial relief.

At the beginning of 1952, the president declared that the United States must build its economic strength to face continuing aggression over a long period—a middle course had to be plotted in response to the conditions of neither total war nor full peace. He outlined these goals: defense objectives had to be reached; production capacity must be expanded; programs in education, health, and social security should be improved; and inflation must be controlled.

Controlling inflation called for efforts in three separate areas. First, fiscal policy was to be geared to increase taxation. (In fact, three tax laws were passed in eighteen months, adding $15 billion in revenues. But that was not enough, and deficits grew in fiscal 1952 and 1953.) Second, restraints were to be imposed on credit, especially by means of selective controls, and full powers were to be restored to the Federal Reserve System to control consumer and housing credit. Third, while the Office of Price Stabilization had made great progress, it needed broader powers.

The Gross National Product, which had increased 15 percent in 1951, increased another 5.5 percent in 1952; unemployment ended the year unchanged, at the probably irreducible minimum of 2.7 percent. Due largely to price controls, along with an abatement of buying pressures as the economy adjusted to war conditions, the Consumer Price Index rose only 1.6 percent in 1952. This success was achieved despite an increase in the money supply of about 5 percent and a budget deficit of $5.8 billion. Credit policy was more active, and in 1952 the interest rate for ninety-day Treasury bills reached 1.77 percent and the Federal Reserve discount rate, 2 percent. Nonetheless, the degree of credit restraint exercised through increases in interest rates was slight.

At the beginning of 1953, the president devoted part of his fiscal Economic Report to a review of progress under the Employment Act of 1946. He emphasized its bipartisan character and said it provided a framework for policy coordination. The act dealt successfully with the 1949 recession and had alerted the government to inflationary pressures. Its basic economic principles were to encourage full employment, to balance the economy, to coordinate economic planning, and to avoid inflation. Considering today's inflationary trends, the unflagging emphasis of the Truman administration on anti-inflationary policies was a successful chapter in our economic history.

The supply of energy was, understandably, not a preoccupation of the Truman administration. But one can find in the president's 1949 Economic Report (CEA section) the opinion that it was unlikely that atomic energy or energy generated by sunlight, wind, and tides would play a significant role in the next few years; but, the report continued, these areas deserved continuing exploration and development in view of the exhaustible character of mineral fuels. Finally, the Economic Report advanced a sound conservation policy, encouraging the use of water power and coal in place of oil and gas.

In retrospect, I believe that during the Truman administration the tax structure served the purposes of the American people well. Despite the additional tax burdens, the American people enjoyed a higher standard of living than ever before. Production increased and future productive capacity expanded. The experience of the Truman years demonstrated our real capacity to exercise self-discipline by using taxation wisely. That period generated confidence that a courageous and constructive approach to tax policy can help build a sound and enduring prosperity.

The six and a half years following June 1946, when I became secretary of the treasury, were a time of rapid evolution in America's international financial policies, designed to meet changing political and economic developments around the world. We first passed through a postwar adjustment to the termination of lend-lease arrangements and through the period of emphasis on the physical recovery of our industrial and agricultural production. Then in 1949 and 1950, we gave increased attention to financial, monetary, and exchange policies that would lead to the kind of international monetary system and level of international trade we had been seeking. The attack on the Republic of Korea in 1950 spurred new emphasis on defense throughout the free world and presented new problems in America's financial relationships with other countries.

As secretary of the treasury throughout this period, while dealing with the immediate and urgent problems which arose daily, I kept before the world our broad objective of greater international trade and investment to improve the standard of living of the free peoples and to attain increased production, employment, and trade. Because of the expense of our foreign assistance programs, I encouraged a greater reliance on trade and investment and a better balance in international accounts (to be achieved through realistic exchange rates backed up by sound internal financial policies in the countries participating in our assistance programs). In short, I wanted to see an expansion of multilateral trade and a greater degree of convertibility of currencies. These two developments would open the world to the stimulating and constructive forces of a competitive price system operating internationally as well as domestically. Accordingly, the United States sought the removal of all hampering restrictions—whether they took the form of restrictive tariffs, quotas, prohibitions, exchange restrictions, or other artificial supports or devices.

The United States contributed markedly to the success in attaining these objectives. We maintained a strong currency, and through our free convertibility of dollars into gold for international transactions, we provided the foundation upon which the world monetary system could be rebuilt. We made substantial progress in reducing our barriers to the free flow of international commerce, by lowering our tariffs and improving our customs administration. I was pleased with the results. Our imports grew significantly, and our friends abroad, by trading freely in world markets, were able to pay more of their own way.

Since much of this progress depended on the actions of other governments, I led our efforts to obtain their cooperation. I traveled widely, and I encouraged constant contacts between the Treasury Department and foreign finance ministers. My travels took me to Latin America in 1946, 1947, and 1952; to the Middle East and the Far East in 1949; and to Europe in 1949, 1950, and 1952. The ultimate decisions in exchange, fiscal, and other financial matters were, of course, in the hands of the countries concerned, but we were able to seek their cooperation and to express our views.

In addition to the normal relations between governments, we had, in the International Monetary Fund, an organization that promoted consultation and cooperation concerning exchange policies. Throughout my term as secretary of the treasury, I served as IMF governor for the United States and appreciated the opportunity to take an active part both in its early formative stages and in its subsequent development.

I was also chairman of the National Advisory Council on International Monetary and Financial Problems, which Congress charged with coordinating international grants and credits. The council reviewed the issues of financial policy raised by the annual assistance programs, as well as those problems presented by the continuing operations of national and international lending agencies.

After the aggression in Korea, the Treasury was concerned with the financial aspects of our mutual security programs. As these programs developed under the aegis of NATO, it became apparent that many of the major policy decisions in foreign countries could be taken only with the active participation and approval of the finance ministers. Frequently the critical questions concerned the financial effort required of NATO members—both in relation to the contributions of other members and in relation to the form and amount of American assistance. At the same time, the extent of our contribution was a matter of major concern to taxpayers. Accordingly, at the designation of the president, I became a member of the NATO Council, serving in this capacity with the secretary of state and the secretary of defense.

A special responsibity arose from the Korean conflict. In support of our efforts there, I took action on December 17, 1950, to block financial transactions involving either Communist China or North Korea. This measure not only immobilized existing dollar assets of Communist China and North Korea and their nationals, but prevented them from selling their goods in this country to finance their attack on our forces.

When I began my term as secretary of the treasury in June 1946, along with the problem of immediate postwar relief and reconstruction, we were faced with the task of building a stronger international monetary system. An initial step was continuation of the financial institutions that had originated in the 1944 Bretton Woods Conference. One of these was the International Monetary Fund, designed to improve its members' standard of living and to promote production and trade through international cooperation in exchange and convertible currencies. To this end, the IMF was provided with funds available for short-term financial assistance, to be associated with its consultations and review of the exchange, monetary, and financial policies of its members. The second new institution, the International Bank for Reconstruction and Development, was designed to make or guarantee international loans for productive purposes.

The year 1947 was marked by increasing evidence that many foreign countries, particularly in Europe, were unable to convert to peacetime conditions and to carry out needed reconstruction without serious inflation and a critical strain on their balance of payments. The immediate postwar relief program began to be replaced by American recovery programs. These were developed by the executive branch and presented to Congress in the winter of 1947–48.

Following Secretary [of State George C.] Marshall's now-famous speech proposing the plan that would eventually bear his name, agencies of the government began to formulate a program of assistance to the European countries. The National Advisory Council gave extended consideration to the financial terms upon which aid should be extended and to the obligations that participating countries should assume as a condition to receiving aid. As chairman of the National Advisory Council, I presented its recommendations on these matters to the appropriate congressional committees. After a year's experience with the program, I again appeared before the committees with additional recommendations. In each of the successive years of the Truman administration, the financial terms of the aid programs were considered by the council, and its recommendations formed an important part of the administration's program. The Marshall Plan legislation made the administrator for economic cooperation a member of the council, thus ensuring that the European Recovery Program would be fully coordinated with the other international financial policies and programs of the United States.

From this brief review of Treasury policies and programs, it should be clear that postwar conditions required extraordinary efforts. Revenues during the Truman years more than paid for government expenditures. Confidence in the credit of the government was maintained. Within the Treasury Department, and in cooperation with other units of the government, a great many steps were taken to improve operating practices and to provide better service to the public at a minimum cost. In the international arena, our government successfully met the challenge of providing effective leadership in the new international financial organizations, effective aid to our allies in their struggle to rebuild their economies and their international trade, and effective cooperation with other free nations in a program of mutual defense against aggression. Many problems still remained, the major one being the continuing Communist threat. The progress made during the Truman years, however, provided a strong basis for future endeavors to promote a lasting peace.

5

The Role of
The Labor Department

David A. Morse

World War II shattered the myth that the United States could isolate itself from the rest of the world, and subsequent international political, economic, and social developments highlighted the ways in which our domestic and foreign policies were becoming intertwined. This was particularly true in the arenas of economics and of labor. America's expanded global role and the growing importance of labor as an economic and political force (both at home and abroad) contributed to our increasing interest in having expert knowledge of foreign and domestic labor affairs.

During the reconversion period (1945 to 1948), the Labor Department was primarily concerned with supporting the president's policies to promote and maintain a strong, stable economy. Domestically, of course, it was necessary to ensure prosperity and a decent standard of living. Internationally, a strong economy would enable us to help Europe, whose recovery we saw as vital to our own political and economic future. Should the economic and political vacuums of a devastated Europe be filled by totalitarian forces, we felt that the foundation of American democracy would be threatened and our future economic and political relations with Western Europe jeopardized.

Domestically, the Labor Department promoted administration programs to develop three elements essential to economic stability: high productivity; a balanced wage-price relationship and controlled inflation; and stable labor-management relations through free collective bargaining.

High productivity was one of the major economic objectives outlined in the Employment Act of 1946. Its premise was that a sustained, increased level of production was the key to maintaining high employment, reasonable prices, and a constantly improving standard of living. Between 1946 and 1948, productivity was extremely high; indeed, in 1947 we reached the unprecedented level of employment of 60 million jobs. Unemployment—2.7 percent, or about 2 million people—was close to the level recognized as unavoidable in a free and mobile economy. We were not afraid that limited manpower or job availability would hinder production. We were most concerned that the wage-price spiral and the serious inflation rate—which was touched off by the relaxation of wage, price, and production controls almost immediately after V-J Day—would not only keep us from meeting our objectives but would also spell economic collapse.

There was a great deal of controversy surrounding the causes of inflation, with price increases often attributed to previous wage increases. It is true that direct controls on wages were the first to be relaxed and also that until mid 1946, wage increases overtook price increases. But it must be remembered that the first round of postwar wage increases (15 percent) was necessary to compensate for the postwar decline in many workers' take-home pay. These workers— who had voluntarily gone without significant raises during the war and who were eager to share in the fruits of the victory for which they had worked so hard—found their weekly earnings were significantly lower after the war. The number of working hours per week was reduced; there was no more overtime; and peacetime jobs often paid less. Thus, the 15 percent adjustments were intended to offset the decline in income.

The end of rationing in 1945 had unleashed a surge of consumer demand that had been suppressed during the war. The one-month lapse of the price-control law (from June to July 1946) brought the most rapid monthly increase in prices ever recorded up to that time in the United States. During that one month, the Wholesale Price Index [WPI] (based on the 1926 average) increased 11.8 percent—from 112.9 percent to 124.7 percent; similarly, the Consumer Price Index (based on the 1935 to 1939 average) climbed 7.9 percent—from 133.3 percent to 141.2 percent.

The lifting of major price controls in October 1946 again sent prices and the cost of living spiraling. By December 1946 the WPI had climbed another 15.3 percent, to 140 percent, and the CPI was up 12.1 percent, to 153.3 percent. Because food prices accounted for the major portion of the CPI's increase, the cost of living rose dramatically. By October 1946 the exorbitant price of meat had made it so scarce that there were no current prices to be included in the CPI, and August prices had to be used!

Although price increases were related to wage increases, Department of Labor figures showed that by mid 1946 price increases clearly exceeded the level attributable to wage increases. The increase in prices and the cost of living had become so great that the wage gains of 1945 and early 1946 were virtually offset—and in the case of the low-wage earner, overshadowed. Therefore, a second round of wage increases was initiated in February 1946 to catch up with the escalating cost of living.

We at the Labor Department did not agree with those who called for the end of price controls, arguing that increased production and the satisfaction of pent-up demands would lead, if not to a reduction, at least to a stabilization of prices. This theory quickly proved itself false. Between mid 1946 and mid 1947 the price of fuel increased 13 percent; clothing, 19 percent; and retail food prices, 40 percent. By mid 1947 the overall cost of living had increased 23 percent; clearly, we were in our second round of inflation. And just as clearly, the alarming price increases and rife speculation on the commodity markets made it apparent that immediate action had to be taken by the government to curtail further price increases. For these reasons we in the Labor Department fully supported and welcomed President Truman's decision to bring Congress back, on November 17, for a special session to deal with the problem of inflation.

It was our contention that if runaway prices could be held down, wage demands would adapt themselves accordingly. Our criterion was real wages and what money could buy, not an amount on a paycheck. Controlling wages through the control of prices was the cornerstone of our policy recommendations to the president.

In his November 17 statement, President Truman announced a ten-point plan, which became the basis of his anti-inflation campaign over the next several years. It included several Labor Department suggestions. First, we proposed authorizing the government to prepare for price and distribution control over any commodities that were then, or were likely to be, in short supply to prevent inadequate inventories of essential foodstuffs. This would allow us to meet both domestic demand and the requirements of our foreign aid program. Second, we proposed that the government be granted authority to limit the domestic use of commodities and to require that any in short or limited supply be set aside. This not would not only assure adequate supplies but would also restrain prices by curtailing demand. Third, we recommended extending the authority of the government and the Federal Reserve Board to control the expansion of consumer and industrial credit, and we also recommended extending government authority to curb speculation on the commodity exchanges. Fourth, we supported continuation of export controls beyond the March 1948 expiration date of the current law. This would prevent depletion of our stocks of essential commodities needed for the European Recovery Plan and for other foreign policy objectives. Fifth, we recommended incentives to induce farmers to market livestock at a lighter weight and thus to conserve grain. Sixth, we favored the extension of rent controls as a major component in stabilizing the cost of living. (In the three months following relaxation of controls under the Rent Control Act of 1947, rents increased more than they had in the previous eight years—a fact that reinforced our position.) Lastly, the Labor Department recommended that government strongly dissuade another round of wage increases. We also suggested, however, that statutory or administrative wage controls not be imposed. Based on the previous years' experience, we felt that a third round of wage increases would merely precipitate a third round of price increases, offsetting the gains won by organized labor and diminishing the purchasing power of unorganized workers.

Although we discouraged a general round of wage increases, for workers at the low end of the wage structure, whose real earning lagged behind increases in the cost of living, we urged that wages be increased. The Labor Department had taken this position since 1946 and was strongly behind President Truman's calls for a revision of the Fair Labor Standards Act to increase the minimum wage to seventy-five cents per hour. Although conditions had changed since 1938 when that act set a forty-cent wage, the principle of establishing a minimum standard of welfare and economic well-being had not. Reports from the Bureau of Labor Statistics showed that in 1947 a seventy-five cent minimum was necessary to maintain the same relationship to the general level of wages and prices that forty cents had represented in 1938. It was a matter of economic justice; it would benefit 1.5 million workers; and in most cases it represented only a slight cost to employers.

About a week after the special session opened, I met with Charles Murphy, the assistant to the president who was responsible for writing the anti-inflation message. We both felt that the president's program was in the best interest of the country and of labor in particular, as labor was always hit hardest by inflation. We agreed that food prices should be tackled first, in the hope that if they were controlled, labor would exercise restraint and not ask for large wage increases. I emphasized, however, that measures taken to decrease food prices should not interfere with the maximum agricultural production needed both to satisfy our domestic demand and to fulfill our foreign obligations to the European Recovery Program.

The president's program was based on the premise of intensive voluntary action on the part of both producers and consumers. Murphy and I agreed that if the measures proposed by the president were adopted, the government's commitment to restrain prices might dampen wage demands and make specific controls unnecessary. I expressed my concern that labor not be asked to bear the full brunt of inflation and said that I felt we could ask labor to voluntarily withhold its demands for further wages only if there were some check on prices. Murphy assured me that labor would not have to shoulder the full responsibility for exercising voluntary restraint, but he also indicated that workers would not be allowed to upset the applecart by demanding large wage increases.

Another crucial component of our economic and political success during the Truman years was the maintenance of stable labor-management relations. We had all seen the effects of the nationwide strikes between V-J Day and June 1946 when 4,650 work stoppages—involving 5,088,000 men and 116,600,000 man-hours—crippled production and threatened our economic viability. We in the Labor Department felt that these disputes did not arise because of ineffectual government policies or machinery or because of the inability of collective bargaining to resolve labor problems. Instead, we saw these work stoppages as a natural part of the difficult process of reconversion—not only reconversion from war to peace but also reconversion from the settlement of disputes by the government (through the National War Labor Board) back to the process of collective bargaining. The workers—who had remained loyal and steadfast during the war and who were fearful of coming unemployment, concerned about decreases in take-home pay, and disconcerted by talk of impending dislocations—were eager to secure benefits while they could. In addition, the collective bargaining skills of labor and management alike were a little rusty. After all, the war interrupted the practice of collective bargaining which had barely had time to test its wings since passage of the Wagner Act in 1935.

Our contention that the labor disputes were a temporary phase of adjustment was borne out by the resumption in early 1947 of stable, peaceful labor-management relations. Free collective bargaining was relied on to negotiate union contracts, and large or lengthy work stoppages were avoided. We believed that the solution to labor-management problems would not be found by legislating a role for government. It was our opinion that free and voluntary collective bargaining best promoted industrial peace and that the role of the government was to assure the greatest possible equality of each side. We also felt that to foster peaceful and stable industrial relations, the causes of economic insecurity to the worker had to be removed. For these reasons we supported the president in his repeated calls for extended social security, unemployment compensation, better housing, and national health insurance.

We also strongly supported President Truman's State of the Union address of 1947 which outlined a four-point program to reduce industrial strife. The program included the extension of facilities in the Department of Labor to assist collective bargaining, a broadened program of social legislation to alleviate the causes of workers' insecurity, creation of a Temporary Joint Commission to inquire into the field of labor-management relations, and legislation to prevent such unjustifiable practices as jurisdictional strikes or secondary boycotts.

Unfortunately, the public did not believe that the strikes were just a temporary product of the readjustment process and was eager to avoid any future disruptions. The conservative Republican Eightieth Congress was equally eager to restain labor and return to the days before the Wagner Act. The Taft-Hartley Act, which came out of that Congress, proved to be one of the most crucial issues for labor and consumed a great deal of the Labor Department's time.

Although most of the cabinet supported the bill, Secretary [of Labor Lewis B.] Schwellenbach and I were adamantly in opposition and urged the president to oppose it. The bill was bad for labor, for management, and for the country. It weakened unions and undermined the national policy of collective bargaining, established under the Wagner Act. It signaled a return to settling labor disputes by injunction and injected the government into private economic affairs on a new level, impeding many of our democratic principles. It also would not accomplish what it was supposed to: specifically, prevent nationwide strikes and aid in achieving the equitable and early settlement of disputes in vital industries. The fact that the Taft-Hartley Act overturned many of the security clauses in existing contracts meant that a new basis of agreement would have to be found, a process that would, in itself, inevitably entail a long struggle and industrial unrest.

Perhaps most repugnant, Taft-Hartley dealt with collective bargaining as if it were a tool working against the public interest and treated management and labor as if they were opponents on contending teams. This was a real step backwards. We had been working to promote the idea that labor and management were associates working together for their own good and for the public good: labor did not benefit when businesses failed; neither could management prosper if low wages kept workers from buying goods. Taft-Hartley not only failed to recognize this, it promoted the opposite view.

I remember that defeating the Taft-Hartley bill was a major preoccupation of an informal group that included myself, Clark Clifford, Oscar Ewing, Leon Keyserling, Charles Murphy, Don Kingsley, and "Jebby" [C. Girard] Davidson. We felt that the president should oppose the bill on two grounds: first, it was detrimental to peaceful labor relations; and second, with labor such a strong Democratic force, it was politically crucial that the president keep its support—not only for his present programs but also with an eye to the 1948 elections.

After the bill was passed, Clark Clifford put the veto proposal before President Truman. I remember that Bill

Foster, undersecretary of commerce, Paul Herzog of the National Labor Relations Board [NLRB], and I were asked to look at the veto statement. We agreed that it would be a mistake for President Truman to do anything but veto the Taft-Hartley Act. Despite the fact that Congress overrode the president's veto, his stand gave him clout with organized labor, with working people in general, and with the liberal section of the Democratic party which had been disaffected. I was in Geneva at the International Labor Organization [ILO] conference when the president delivered his veto message. The reaction was electric, and it enhanced our prestige among those countries who tended to regard the United States as moving to the right.

The international dimension of labor policy was also an important province of the Department of Labor immediately following World War II. The reorganization of the department in 1946 and the subsequent establishment in 1947 of its Office of International Labor Affairs, to coordinate a previously fragmented U.S. foreign policy on labor, not only reinforced the view that labor had become a potent economic and political force internationally, but also acknowledged that foreign and domestic labor developments were interrelated.

On July 1, 1946, I was appointed as the first assistant secretary of labor for international affairs. I was the first to hold this title; before, all international matters had been handled on an ad hoc basis. My responsibilities included coordinating and supervising the international work of the various Labor Department bureaus and divisions and speaking for the department on international matters. I acted as advisor to the United States delegate to the United Nations Economic and Social Council and its commissions. I was in charge of all ILO activities, including being the United States representative to the ILO and chief of the United States delegation to the International Labor Conference. In addition, I served on the Board of the Foreign Service, the Executive Committee on Economic Foreign Policy, the Interdepartmental Committee on International

Social Policy, and the Advisory Committee on Occupied Areas.

The Foreign Service Act of 1946, in granting statutory membership to the Department of Labor on the Board of the Foreign Service, really marked the beginning of the recognition of Labor's rightful involvement in and concern with international affairs. Up until that time, the department was really not involved in the international arena, and there had been little or no contact between Labor and other departments concerning foreign policy.

As the Labor Department's representative on the Board of the Foreign Service, I pushed particularly hard for the expansion and improvement of the labor attaché program. The Departments of Commerce and Agriculture already had numerous attachés assigned to missions throughout the world, and I felt it was necessary that Labor be given equal representation for two reasons. First, the decided impact of labor developments abroad on our domestic situation increased the need for international information. Second, the increased importance of labor as a nascent economic and political force—particularly in wartorn and occupied areas, vulnerable to influence of any sort—made it necessary that the United States government have complete, accurate, and timely reporting on labor affairs. This would enable the Labor Department to contribute effectively to our foreign policy.

My experience during the war at the Supreme Headquarters of the Allied Expeditionary Forces [SHAEF] as an advisor on labor policy and programs for what was to become the military governments in occupied areas convinced me of the necessity of good intelligence information. I saw that the new free trade unions developing in Europe would play a key role in the formation of postwar democratic institutions and policies and were therefore crucial to our future relations, both political and economic. I felt it was vital that there be United States attachés with experience in the labor field to monitor labor developments and keep our government informed.

The promotion of free democratic trade unions in the occupied areas of Germany and Austria—and Korea and Japan as well—was one of the major concerns of the Office of International Labor Affairs. Our efforts were conducted primarily through the Advisory Committee on Occupied Areas; through liaison activities between the Departments of State, War, and Labor; and with the support of the Trade Union Advisory Committee on International Affairs. Because the Truman administration believed that democratic institutions could best be fostered by indigenous elements, not by foreigners, and by example and interaction, rather than by edict and inculcation, we set up a series of exchange programs that brought trade union leaders (from Germany, in particular) to meet with American labor leaders, to discuss labor problems, and to see our system in action.

The Trade Union Advisory Committee on International Affairs [TUAC] was one of the most significant and effective of these policy groups. During the postwar years, the labor movement was split, and the American Federation of Labor [AFL] and the Congress of Industrial Organizations [CIO] were not even on speaking terms. As hard as it was to try and get labor and management together to solve domestic problems, it was equally difficult to get the unified support of labor on international issues. In order to develop some kind of consensus on international policy, I thought it might be worthwhile to get the top labor leaders together regularly to discuss the interests of labor in international relations and what course our government should follow. This led to creation of the TUAC in December 1946; its members at that time were broadly representative of the American labor movement.

The TUAC actually served a dual purpose. First, by bringing together the top trade union leaders, putting the issues on the table and asking them what they thought, the administration was getting first-hand information on the interests and needs of American labor. This was important because we needed to know that we were not operating in a vacuum when we spoke on behalf of American labor in international areas. Second, TUAC enabled us to develop a consensus and to marshal labor's support behind President Truman's foreign programs so that we appeared united when we spoke beyond the three-mile limit.

TUAC support was particularly crucial in winning acceptance of the Truman Doctrine. Prior to its announcement by President Truman, Dean Acheson—then undersecretary of state—got hold of me and said it was absolutely essential that we have the support of both the AFL and the CIO. President Truman was concerned that the vacuum created by the British withdrawal from Greece and Turkey and the Greek civil war would be filled by Communist groups. The AFL, which was virulently anti-Communist, would have no trouble supporting this. The CIO, however, at that time maintained close relations with the World Federation of Trade Unions [WFTU] which had Communist leanings. Dean Acheson agreed to come to a special private session of the TUAC and give a briefing on the importance of the Truman Doctrine to U.S. foreign policy. We convinced all the labor leaders, despite their differences on other matters, to support the program when the president announced it publicly.

The Marshall Plan, of course, was another significant development of the Truman years and perhaps most vividly exemplified the interrelationship of foreign and domestic economic and political policies. After World War II, Europe was devastated and could not stand on its own feet. The United States, on the other hand, had the material and the physical resources to help with the European recovery. Any instability or deterioration in our own economy would not only have threatened our domestic reconversion, it would have made foreign aid impossible. Conversely, preserving Europe's economic health was in our interest as well. We saw Europe's recovery and economic vitality—by fostering an economic and political climate conducive to the expansion of democratic trade unions and democratic governments —as insurance against the threat of totalitarianism and loss of liberty that befell war-ravaged countries too economically desperate to resist Communist pressures.

At the specific request of the president, the Labor Department supported the Marshall Plan wholeheartedly. I made numerous appearances throughout the country to elicit labor's support for the plan; on important occasions Paul Hoffman, the first administrator of the Marshall Plan, appeared with me. The purpose was to have him become well acquainted with the labor movement and to enable us to mobilize support for this great effort. Labor was encouraged to contribute to the stability of the American economy for international as well as national purposes. I think that the success of the Marshall Plan ensured that the international labor movement would continue as a free and democratic force; these democratic institutions helped save Europe, a great economic and political accomplishment.

6

The Economics of Agriculture

Charles F. Brannan

Early in his administration, President Truman said: "Prosperous farmers make for a prosperous nation; and when farmers are in trouble, the nation is in trouble." This is a very concise statement of the economic policy he consistently followed and implemented as president: with his knowledge and approval, the Department of Agriculture used its legislative clout to maintain the prices farmers received for agricultural products and livestock at fair levels—or as farmers say, at parity. Prices to farmers remained well above parity throughout the Truman administration, by an annual expenditure of appreciably less than $1 billion. In comparison, farm prices promptly began to decline after his term expired and fell far below parity; meanwhile the cost of farm programs rose from less than $1 billion in 1952 to over $6 billion in 1959.

President Truman's concern for farmers, however, was not limited to guaranteeing fair prices for the various crops that made possible our enviably high standard of living. He also understood the importance, as well as the justice, of providing farm families with at least an opportunity to enjoy an income comparable to that of fellow citizens in other walks of life. Therefore, with the president's encouragement, a new proposal was developed by the Department of Agriculture to permit a farmer to earn a fair and justifiable income from the reasonably efficient operation of an average-sized farm, without placing an undue burden on the U.S.

Treasury. This proposal was presented to an extraordinary joint session of the House and Senate Agricultural Committees on April 7, 1949.

The plan set off a nationwide debate on agricultural policy, a debate sometimes more political than economic in its overtones. Farmers, farm organization leaders, consumers, food processors and retailers, labor unions, churchmen, and a host of others joined in the debate. The plan was also caught up in the McCarthyism of the era: it was promptly labeled "socialistic" and "communistic." One congressman claimed he had proof, supplied by the Farm Bureau, that the author of the plan had received it directly from Moscow. But this didn't bother Mr. Truman at all. Rep. Steve Pace of Georgia, the ranking Democrat on the House Agriculture Committee, introduced a bill providing for a trial run of the Agriculture Department's plan, applicable to producers of a selected group of perishables. But the bill was defeated by a coalition of Northern Republicans and some Southern Democrats.

There are those who maintain that the plan would have been adopted had not the Korean War erupted and reversed the decline in farm prices. With the war's boost—and the shortages it created—that great rugged individualist, the American farmer, decided he really did not need any government assistance after all. Nevertheless, the plan fostered a glorious fight, and for a decade or more, its proposals continued to inject themselves into serious discussions of the unresolved economic problems in agriculture.

A detailed description or analysis of the plan is not possible here. But some familiarity with a few of its provisions is necessary to understand the extraordinary controversy it engendered and, in particular, to evaluate its potential for curbing today's inflationary spiral.

The plan set forth a formula for determining parity from year to year—what were fair and reasonable prices for each crop. The prices actually received by farmers in the marketplace would depend on the free operation of the law of supply and demand. But if the average of all prices received by all farmers for a specific crop during a normal marketing season was less than the fair price (as determined by the new formula), the government would make up the difference. This payment would go directly to each producer of the crop. Based on the number of units of the crop he marketed, a farmer would get an amount equal to the difference between the average unit price received by all producers of that crop during the marketing season and the fair price. (There was one limitation which I will discuss below.)

For example, assume that the predetermined fair price for wheat in a particular marketing season was $3.50 a bushel and that the average price received by all wheat producers that season was only $3 a bushel. Obviously some farmers received less than the average $3 per bushel and others received more. Then assume that some less efficient farmers, who produced an inferior grade of wheat or marketed it carelessly, received only $2.80 per bushel (20 cents less than the national average), while other farmers, who produced a superior product and marketed it wisely, received $3.20 per bushel (20 cents more than the national average). Shortly after the end of the marketing season all wheat producers who had sold wheat that season would receive a payment of 50 cents for each bushel marketed—the amount being the difference between the national average price of $3 for that marketing season and the predetermined fair price of $3.50. The less efficient farmer would receive $2.80 per bushel for his crop at the grain elevator, plus 50 cents from the government—a total of $3.30 per bushel. The efficient farmer would receive $3.20 per bushel at the elevator, plus 50 cents from the government, making a total of $3.70 per bushel for his crop. Thus, in addition to providing the farmer with a fair return for his investment in land, equipment, seed, and fertilizer and for his labor and skill, the proposal created a monetary incentive to farm efficiently and to market carefully.

It may be difficult to assess the extent to which such a payment to farmers would be reflected in the price that consumers pay for a finished product. For example, when the price farmers receive for their wheat declines, there is seldom a corresponding decline in the price consumers pay for bread. On the other hand, increases in the price of bread are regularly explained and justified by an increase in the price of wheat. Consumers often do see a reflection, however, of changes in the prices paid to farmers for perishable products such as meat and vegetables. Nevertheless, under this plan the spread between the price of the raw materials to the initial producer and the price paid by the ultimate consumer would be far more exposed to public view and analysis than it is today; and the burden of justifying the spread would rest squarely with the handlers, the processors, and the retailers.

Under existing agricultural programs, the government was already spending large sums of money through non-recourse loans and heavy administrative costs to maintain the price of farm products to producers (and consumers) at artificially high levels. The plan we proposed in 1949 would cut overhead and pay the required portion directly to the producers.

Explicit in the government's proposed assurance to farmers of a fair return was a reciprocal obligation: farmers were to help make the program workable and to keep the government's cost within reasonable limits. Therefore, the program provided that if the previous year's production of any crop substantially exceeded genuine demand for all purposes, each farmer would curtail his production or his marketing (or both) of that crop on an equitable pro-rata base with all other producers.

It was an important advance. By statute, at the time this plan was introduced, there continued to be high price supports for many food commodities, with production stimulated by price incentives for war and postwar requirements. The result was grossly excessive supplies of several crops and a correspondingly excessive and needless burden on the U.S. Treasury. It also constituted an indefensible waste of agricultural resources. The postwar price support for potatoes, a highly perishable crop, was a glaring example. After buying and paying farmers $6 or more per hundred-weight for potatoes, the government resold a hundred-pound sack for about the price of the burlap bag and then paid the freight to transport the potatoes to the purchaser, in some cases a distillery, many miles away.

Our 1949 plan also took into account the very real probability that direct payments to farmers would encourage them to buy more land. This would lead to an unsettling inflation in the price of farmland and would stimulate the trend toward concentration of farmlands into fewer and fewer units. Therefore, the plan included a recommendation that the total amount of direct payments to any single farm operation for all its production would be limited. Furthermore, the production of any farm in excess of a predetermined amount would be ineligible for these direct payments. The operators of all farms, no matter how large, would participate in the direct-payment program, but their payments were not to exceed a specific dollar amount. This became known as the family farm cutoff, and it was a rather bold recommendation at that time. (This concept, however, has since been included in a number of bills extending the present farm price-support program.)

The method of determining the upper limit of a direct payment to any one farm was computed by taking a historic average annual gross return from the sale of all crops from a typical large family farm. Such a farm would be modern, mechanized, efficiently operated and might use some hired labor during peak work periods. But primarily it would be a farm on which the farmer accepted full responsibility for management and one on which he and his family did the bulk, if not all, of the work.

This recommendation for a family farm cutoff rested on the premise that there is a genuine public interest, if not a responsibility of government, in providing a reasonably diligent farmer with an opportunity to earn a fair return for his contribution to the national economy and welfare. The same principle underlies the minimum wage, the Wagner Act, and many other pieces of national legislation. But there is no public interest in encouraging big producers to get bigger at the taxpayer's expense. No one can object to a producer expanding his resources and output by his own efforts, but contributing tax dollars for that objective is not a public responsibility. This feature of the plan, as finally presented, clearly evidenced President Truman's concern about the welfare and the future of family farms.

After the proposal had been examined and tested by Department of Agriculture economists and leaders of farm organizations and reviewed by the White House staff, the plan went to the president for his final consideration before being presented to Congress. He reviewed each item, one by one, and the economic, social, and political implications were carefully examined. When the proposal for the family farm cutoff was discussed, I advised the president that this section would probably draw harsh criticism from our political enemies and suggested that therefore he might wish to eliminate it.

Mr. Truman read the section two or three times, then he looked up at me and said, "But Charlie, it's right, isn't it?"

I responded that I believed it was right. He thought a minute and said, "It stays in."

The section stayed in—and we caught all the abuse that we expected.

Overall, the plan had many parts. For example, direct payments would not help farmers who because of adverse weather had no harvest; hence, a comprehensive crop insurance program was recommended. Neither would direct payments help farmers with inadequate resources; therefore, a credit program was proposed to help the members of this group acquire adequate-sized family farms.

Implicit in the plan was the notion that once farmers had a reasonable assurance of earning a fair return on their investment (in land, equipment, supplies, labor, and skills), they would be in a financial position to improve their farms without the additional financial assistance they now received from the government.

As we all know, the plan was never adopted by Congress, although some portions of it appear in various pieces of farm legislation, even today. In particular, the early sugar program had many similarities, and the original wool-support legislation provided for direct payments but lacked the family farm cutoff.

When the plan was first introduced in 1949, little attention was given to its anti-inflationary potential: inflation simply was not a major problem then. However, by 1957 the signs were beginning to appear in some areas of the economy. Economist John Kenneth Galbraith recognized the inflationary trend in food prices and suggested direct payments to farmers as an effective tool for curtailing it. In an article in the *Atlantic* entitled "Are Living Costs out of Control?" Galbraith wrote, "A change in farm policy from the system of pegging farm prices to one of allowing them to find their own level, with the farmers' income protected by direct payments, would be immensely useful in attacking inflation."

Throughout the national debate on the plan, the fact that consumers as well as farmers would benefit from its direct-payment program was strongly emphasized. But the argument was not very persuasive to Congress. The idea of rewarding American farmers for their remarkable production during and after the war with depressed prices and incomes was clearly unacceptable to most members of Congress. But the existing system of price supports, which reached into citizens' pockets twice, using their taxes to keep their food prices artificially high, was not sufficiently disturbing to Congress to warrant adopting the 1949 plan. Similarly, the opportunity to increase our exports of agricultural products by being able to offer them at more competitive prices on the world market was generally ignored. So we continued to pay American exporters an exports subsidy, enabling them to buy grain at the artificially high U.S. price and to reduce their selling price on the world market.

In my judgment, the economic policies of the Truman administration were not only right for the period, in principle, most of them are equally applicable today. Furthermore, if some of those policies had been adopted when proposed, this country could have avoided many of the economic problems which now confront us.

7

Conservation, Public Power, And Natural Resources

C. Girard Davidson

Harry Truman took great pride in his hometown of Independence, Missouri. The Oregon Trail and the wagons of the Mormon trek went through Independence and so did the Missouri floods: it was a crossroads of America. Truman was especially proud of the city-owned electric system because the rates in Independence were cheaper than those of the big private utility in nearby Kansas City. It is not surprising that he developed an interest in electric power and a sympathy for public power. He was the last president to campaign from the back of a railroad car, and he made the most of it. In hundreds of whistle-stop speeches across the country, Truman praised small towns, and to him they were all like Independence.

His ten years in the Senate (he was first elected in 1934) provided much of the education and background for his economic policies as president. In 1935 Truman served on the Interstate Commerce Committee chaired by Sen. Burton K. Wheeler of Montana. Truman helped investigate the propaganda activities of the private-power holding companies, exposing the financial manipulations that resulted in many people losing their life savings. He helped President Roosevelt in the battle for passage of the Rayburn-Wheeler bill. By one vote it became the Public Utility Holding Company Act of 1935, one of the major, hard-fought victories of the New Deal.

In looking at the broad spectrum of Truman's economic

policies, particularly those that relate to conservation, public power, and natural resources, rural electrification deserves our attention. His record in that area is significant and has been neglected by historians. During his ten years in the Senate, Truman witnessed the incipient stages of the Rural Electrification Administration's [REA] organization and program. In 1935 only one farm in ten had electricity. During the first decade of REA the percentage of electrified farms rose rapidly, reaching the more fortunate rural people who lived near cities: by early 1945 rural electrification had risen to 46 percent. But the remaining job was much harder.

Nevertheless, during Truman's eight years, REA had its golden age. More than 1.5 million farms and rural places were hooked up. By the end of 1952 more than 85 percent of America's rural areas had electricity. President Truman summarized his satisfaction with rural electrification in a special message to Congress on January 19, 1953, his last full day in office. Entitled "The Nation's Land and Water Resources," it is a message worth reading today because so much of the agenda that President Truman outlined to Congress still remains undone. The occasion for the message was the transmittal of the Cooke Report on water resources. Morris L. Cooke, an engineer, expert on natural resources and public utilities, and head of the Rural Electrification Administration from 1935 to 1937, had been selected in January 1950 as chairman of the president's Water Resources Policy Commission. The resulting three-volume report had been referred to federal agencies for review. Thus, with the benefit of many comments, the president's special message reflected much consideration and represented the essence of his thinking as he left office.

Mr. Truman pointed with pride to the accomplishments of his administration: 1.5 million farms and rural places electrified; 2.7 million kilowatts of electric generation added by means of federal dams. He cited the benefits of these dams to navigation and flood control. He noted that the federal government had doubled the number of soil-conservation districts during his administration and had built more than twelve thousand miles of electric-transmission lines. Against this background Truman urged Congress to look in the coming years for a more efficient means of re- gional river-basin planning, involving states and local com- munities. He called for better procedures by both the executive branch and the Congress to select the best projects and then to insure fair charges to the beneficiaries.

I have dwelt at length on Truman's special message because it summarizes the president's response to the issues of conservation, public power, and natural resources. For the full record one can consult dozens of his speeches, mes- sages to Congress, and above all the actual programs and their results. During his last two weeks in office, Truman sent messages to the Congress on the state of the union, the budget, and the economy. All these reflect a rising sup- port for the development and conservation of the nation's natural resources.

Since I was—and still am—most directly interested in the Columbia River Basin and the Pacific Northwest, I can be more specific by illustrating the impact of Truman's policies on that one region. Using the Pacific Northwest as a case study, however, is a severe test because Franklin D. Roosevelt was a hard act to follow; but even here Truman acquitted himself with distinction. F.D.R. had ordered the construction of the Bonneville and Grand Coulee dams in 1933. He sponsored creation of the Bonneville Power Ad- ministration in 1937. In 1944 and early 1945 F.D.R. signed authorizations for the Hungry Horse and McNary dams and for the four lower Snake River dams. Perhaps it was in part because F.D.R. had been so protective of the Northwest that in 1947 the Eightieth Congress reacted, concentrating much of its spleen on that region, slashing appropriations, reduc- ing staffs, and actually halting projects already under con- struction. Then came 1948.

In May and June of that year, the Columbia River's third greatest flood caused $103 million in damages. Truman visited the Portland area early in June. Six months later the flow of the Columbia dropped sharply; the region was short of power and had to curtail Christmas lighting. Not the least of the events of 1948 was the impact of Truman's campaign speeches as he took his case to the country.

The 1948 election was crucial. Rep. [George] Dondero (R-Mich.) had made clear in a national magazine article that a Dewey victory would mean decimation of the federal power program and the elimination of the clause which provided that in selling federally generated electric power, preference be given to public bodies and rural electric cooperatives. In view of Dondero's prediction, the Pacific Northwest helped itself immensely by electing Truman.

During his second term, President Truman focused his attention on the Pacific Northwest in a special message to the Congress on April 13, 1949, recommending establishment of a Columbia Valley Administration [CVA]. Although the CVA bills were not reported out of committee, the CVA proposal probably had some influence on the Flood Control Act of May 17, 1950, authorizing a record number of dams in the Pacific Northwest. On May 22 the president sent a special message to Congress complaining about the bill's weaknesses, but noting that he had signed it nevertheless.

In light of the 1948 flood, the Army Corps of Engineers had revised its report on the Columbia River. This led to inclusion in the 1950 legislation of a number of upstream storage projects for flood control as well as for generating power. Unfortunately, however, because of opposition by the private power companies, the key upstream storage dam at Hell's Canyon was not included in the act.

In many ways the 1950 act was the last hurrah. It authorized a record number of dams—Libby, John Day, The Dalles, Priest Rapids, Albeni Falls—and some smaller projects, but it failed to provide comprehensive river development or broad regional economic planning of the kind Truman had envisioned in the CVA.

At the dedication of the Hungry Horse Dam on October 1, 1952, President Truman expressed a sense of foreboding concerning General Eisenhower's attitude towards federal dams. On a visit shortly before becoming a candidate, Ike had admired Hoover Dam. Then two months later he made a campaign speech in Boise charging that construction of federal dams reflected "left-wing government." On the basis of this sudden shift in Eisenhower's views, President Truman told his audience at Hungry Horse that they had better take a good look because if the Republicans were elected, it would be a long time before they would see another new dam like it. That was in 1952.

Six years later Harry Truman came to Portland, Oregon, to make a campaign speech at a dinner for Sen. Wayne Morse. Truman recalled his 1952 warning and pointed to the lack of authorizations for new water projects and the lack of new hydroelectric dams. During those six years, the Eisenhower administration had merely been completing Truman dams, and then only because the Democratic Congress initiated and passed the appropriations.

More than twenty years have passed since Truman's observations. In that time our Columbia River Treaty with Canada has provided some valuable upstream storage to control the Columbia River's floods and to improve the power that is available especially at downstream dams. But when the dams presently under construction are completed, the Columbia River will be only about 52 percent developed. Almost 30 million kilowatts of hydroelectric power remains untapped. Probably half of this potential never will be harnessed due to physical, economic, or environmental problems. Still, 75 percent development of the Columbia, including about 15 million acre-feet of additional upstream storage, is possible. The needed investment would probably be $15 billion.

These figures are rough estimates: there is no government report available to tell us what the goal for Columbia River development should be. A Columbia Valley Administration would have filled this need. Instead we do have the 1976 publication of the former Federal Power Commission [FPC] which lists the developed and undeveloped waterpower sites. It shows that as of December 1975 the water power of the Tennessee River was 87.2 percent harnessed in contrast to the Columbia's 38.6 percent. (This figure will be about 52 percent when the projects presently under way are completed.)

My purpose in presenting these statistics is to try to answer the question of where development of the Columbia River would be today if the Truman policies and attitudes had prevailed during the years since 1952. My guess is that the Columbia would probably be 75 percent developed by now. Instead of the present shortage of electric power in the Pacific Northwest, there would be a comfortable surplus. We would not be relying on scarce and expensive foreign oil to generate electricity. We would be in a better position to plan for irrigation as well as for power and for other uses of the river. In short, the Truman policies applied to our rivers and natural resources would have improved our energy situation, with less dependence on foreign fuel. The nation would also have been enriched by a sound investment in the better development of its water resources.

It is tempting to speculate on what President Truman would do about the oil problem if he were in the White House today. Like steel, oil is essential to every one of our civilian and defense programs.

In the late forties, industry could not expand because of the lack of steel: construction of electric power plants was stopped due to the lack of heavy steel plate; and oil exploration could not proceed because of the lack of steel pipe. In 1948, steel production was 10 million tons short of the actual annual demand, and there was little reason to expect that the situation would improve in one year or even in two. The steel men, being apostles of the scarce market and guaranteed profits, liked it that way and encouraged the shortage.

For example, in 1949 Bethlehem Steel's profits were the highest they had been since 1929, and they were earned on a smaller volume of business than the company had in 1929. In January 1949, right after his reelection, President Truman asked for government loans to expand steel production and relieve the shortage and to construct steel plants with federal funds if private industry failed to meet our needs.

Of course, it did not become necessary for the government to build the steel plants. The Congress did not authorize it and did not need to: the steel companies feared government ownership of steel plants even more than expansion of the industry and somewhat lower profits. The choice was clearcut. At the time of the president's January 1949 message, 88 million tons of steel were being produced annually; by 1951 production had increased to 105 million tons. By 1955 the industry had a production capacity of approximately 126 million tons; the country's steel needs were being taken care of; and the profits of the steel companies had leveled off.

Lest I appear despairing about the future, let me say that the chance is not irretrievably lost. National policy may waver from one administration to another, yet in the long run truth tends to prevail over error. The twenty-year Roosevelt-Truman era lifted the nation to a new and higher plateau of progress and gave us a legacy of hope for constructive government. The country is much the better for the New Deal and Fair Deal accomplishments in conservation, public power, and natural resources. We could still reach 75 percent development of the Columbia River and other rivers. We could improve our soil and rebuild our forests. We are endeavoring to conserve energy, and very soon we must embark on a nationwide drive to conserve precious nonrenewable minerals. Such conservation was recommended in 1952 in the report of the Materials Policy Commission, chaired by William S. Paley, and it is a tragedy that its findings were not implemented. Today our research efforts are probing new forms of energy, and in the West it looks as though geothermal explorations may tap unbelievable resources. Our awareness of the importance of protecting our environment presents an additional challenge.

Different historical times call for different styles. The ebb and flow of social and economic patterns and the un-

alterably scrambled geopolitics of the world all cry for new
and creative thinking.

8

International
Economic and Financial Policies

Frank A. Southard, Jr.

The United States economy emerged from World War II undamaged and highly productive. While substantial reconversion to peacetime was necessary, the economy was ready and able to supply the needs of postwar Europe and Japan and to meet the pent-up demands of the rest of the world as well.

The president in his special message to Congress on September 6, 1945, focused almost exclusively on the urgent task of economic reconversion and its accompanying policy considerations. Only one short section of the message was concerned with world problems, and even less attention was given to our economic and financial policies abroad. Mr. Truman mentioned the need to reach constructive settlements on Lend-Lease obligations; pointed to the prospective establishment of the International Monetary Fund and the International Bank; favored extending the operations of the Export-Import Bank; and urged appropriation of the remainder of the United States contribution to the United Nations Relief and Rehabilitation Administration [UNRRA], totaling $1.375 billion. President Truman said that the United States should "do all that is reasonably possible to help war-torn countries to get back on their feet."

In the field of foreign economic and financial policies the eight years of the Truman administration were the most dynamic of the entire postwar period. In part the policies and programs evolved directly from those of the preceding administration—e.g., Bretton Woods and the main lines of trade policy; in part they were the outgrowth of new conditions and necessities.

In 1947 the "containment" of communism became a major goal of U.S. foreign policy. The view was that, as far as international economic and financial policies were concerned, the most effective way of achieving containment was to help the non-Communist countries raise their standards of living—in particular, to help them restore their own productive facilities and reorient their economic activities.* In practical terms, this involved: (1) giving aid for economic reconstruction, fostering European economic integration, and providing technical and economic assistance to developing countries; (2) furthering nondiscriminatory trade and reducing trade barriers; and (3) restoring and maintaining currency convertibility and eliminating restrictions on payments.

A number of programs and institutions were established to carry out these broad policies. In the area of foreign aid and technical assistance, there was the Anglo-American Financial Agreement (1945–46); the International Bank for Reconstruction and Development (1946); aid to Greece and Turkey (1947, 1948); the European Recovery Program, European economic integration, and the Coal and Steel Community (1948–51); and Point Four, technical assistance (1949). In foreign trade, there was the International Trade Organization and the General Agreement on Tariffs and Trade (1949–50); a policy of nondiscriminatory trade with progressively lowered trade barriers; and the Export-Import Bank. In the area of international financial policy, there was the International Monetary Fund (1946); and the European Payments Union (1948).

The Early Years, 1945–48

At the beginning of the Truman administration, the

---

* See *Survey of United States International Finance* (Princeton University Press, 1951), p. 1.

United States was faced with prostrate allies, devastated enemies, and a world less developed than we, a world that had been starved for industrial imports during the war and lacked any impetus to economic development.

During 1945 two notable actions were taken by the administration. First, the Articles of Agreement of the International Bank for Reconstruction and Development and of the International Monetary Fund entered into force on December 27, 1945, and the two institutions began operations in May 1946. These two Bretton Woods institutions, planned during the war, had the administration's firm support at all times. The Bretton Woods Agreement Act, signed by President Truman on July 31, 1945, provided for a National Advisory Council on International Monetary and Financial Problems. This NAC (under the chairmanship of the secretary of the treasury and including the secretaries of state and commerce, the chairman of the Board of Governors of the Federal Reserve System, and the president of the Export-Import Bank) became the principal coordinating agency in the international economic and financial field during the Truman administration. It was invariably chaired by Secretary of the Treasury John W. Snyder and, operating through meetings of deputies, was concerned with a wide range of policies, including Bank and Fund operations, the European recovery program, and foreign loans.

Second, after bitter debate both in the British Parliament and especially in the U.S. Congress,* the Anglo-American Financial Agreement was passed by Congress on December 6, 1945. It included a loan to the United Kingdom of $3.75 billion and, in complicated language, required the restoration of sterling convertibility. This step was undertaken in mid 1947. But, as could have been anticipated in light of Britain's very large external liabilities and its weak balance-of-payments position, it was a short-lived and costly

---

* Recounted in detail in Richard N. Gardner, *Sterling-Dollar Diplomacy: Anglo-American Collaboration in the Reconstruction of Multi-Lateral Trade* (Oxford: Clarendon Press, 1956), chaps. 10–12.

experiment. Secretary Snyder had the difficult and delicate task of bringing it to an end.

In this early period there were three other U.S. actions aimed at dealing with the world's economic disorder. The first was a major U.S. contribution (about $1.3 billion) to the United Nations Relief and Rehabilitation Administration, which operated to provide emergency assistance of food, shelter, and materials to displaced persons.

The second was designed to assist Greece and Turkey in countering external threats and, especially in the case of Greece, to provide quick economic relief. In two successive years, 1947 and 1948, Congress appropriated funds for those purposes.

The third—and in historical perspective, the most important and remarkable action—was the planning and establishment of the European Recovery Program [ERP]. In a speech made at Harvard on June 5, 1947, Secretary of State George C. Marshall said that Europe's requirements over the next three years were so extensive that without substantial help, "she must . . . face economic, social, and political deterioration of a very grave character." Planning within our government and in Europe proceeded during the rest of 1947; subsequent legislation created the Economic Cooperation Administration [ECA] and committed $5 billion for the year ending April 2, 1949. The European countries created the Organization of European Economic Cooperation [OEEC], and there began a dramatically successful American-European collaboration to restore the economic and financial structure of Europe.

The United States emerged from the war in an overwhelmingly strong economic and financial position. Gold reserves increased each year from 1946 to 1949, and our external net short-term liabilities were negligible. The current-account of our balance of payments showed a large surplus, reaching $11.3 billion in 1947, and was in considerable part financed by the drain of dollar assets in foreign countries. It was, of course, this perilous balance-of-payments position that provided the justification for the ERP. It also gave rise to theorizing about an insolvable "dollar problem." Learned books were written to demonstrate that U.S. economic strength was so dominant that our balance of payments would continue to show a surplus for years to come. It can be said that within the administration, and particularly within the Treasury, this view was not shared.

The Middle Years, 1948–50

The years from 1948 through 1950 saw slow but steady progress in Europe's recovery. By the end of 1949 European output exceeded the prewar level by 5 percent and was 25 percent above the 1947 mark. ERP appropriations continued at about $5 billion annually.

The main lines of U.S. trade policy were clear: to continue the emphasis on freedom from undue restrictions and discrimination which had begun with the Trade Agreements Program in 1933. Under Roosevelt the establishment of an International Trade Organization had been planned to operate in the trade field alongside of the IMF in the financial field. With strong U.S. support, the ITO charter was negotiated in Havana, Cuba, during many months of 1948. Legislation was submitted to Congress in April 1949 to authorize U.S. participation. But the hearings, which did not take place until April 1950, generated strong opposition. On December 6, 1950, the State Department announced that the ITO charter would not be resubmitted to Congress. This was an unwelcome defeat. But, making a virtue of necessity, the U.S. joined other countries in using the General Agreement on Tariffs and Trade [GATT]—which was to have been an interim arrangement pending ITO ratification—and ultimately converting it into an institution. (On the whole, the GATT has performed about as effectively in the difficult field of trade and tariff relations as the ITO would have; and it has seen both the Kennedy and the Tokyo rounds of multilateral trade negotiations through long and difficult courses.)

The ERP-OEEC collaboration in these years continued to operate as the effective engine of European economic

recovery. In 1948 and 1949 U.S. officials began their drive for European economic integration which ultimately was to result in the 1958 Treaty of Rome, establishing the European Economic Community. In October 1948, with strong U.S. support, the Intra-European Payments Scheme was initiated to push the ERP countries toward multilateral payments (and, ultimately, currency convertibility). In the last half of 1950 this gave way to the European Payments Union [EPU]. On October 31, 1949, ECA Administrator Paul Hoffman warned OEEC members that they must make progress toward economic integration or face loss of aid. Within the Truman administration this announcement had been the subject of some debate. While the decision commanded majority support, there were persons who argued the alternative case for pressing forward with freer trade and currency convertibility on a global basis. They expressed the fear that European economic integration would result in a protected trade area that would embrace the former colonial empires and would leave the Western Hemisphere and Japan outside.

In his 1949 inaugural address President Truman laid out a program in which he said: "We must embark on a bold new program for making the benefits of our scientific advances and industrial progress available for the improvement and growth of underdeveloped areas." This was the genesis of the Point Four program of technical assistance which would gather momentum in succeeding years. A month later, in February 1949, the U.S. introduced a resolution in the Economic and Social Council [ECOSOC] calling for the establishment of a technical assistance program in the United Nations.

By this time, it was evident that while a good deal of progress was being made in economic reconstruction, little was being made in breaking out of the old monetary network. Exchange restrictions and agreements on bilateral payments divided the world into a convertible dollar area and an inconvertible nondollar area. Most IMF members had declared as initial par values the exchange rates that

prevailed in 1946 and 1947; it was now becoming evident that their currencies, as a group, were overvalued in relation to the dollar. Early in 1949 Secretary Snyder told the Congress that in view of our foreign aid, the U.S. had a direct concern with European exchange rates. In the IMF the U.S. precipitated an examination of exchange rates. The end result of this and other pressures was the devaluation of sterling and a number of other currencies in September and October 1949. Late in 1948, under the leadership of the secretaries of treasury and war, a stabilization program had been devised for Japan, and in April 1949 a single exchange rate of 360 yen per dollar was established, on the recommendation of the NAC.*

During this period the U.S. was a strong supporter of the par-value system that was included in the IMF Articles of Agreement. Since the currencies of most Fund members were heavily protected by exchange controls, par values varied greatly in their effectiveness. But U.S. officials (and the financial officials of most other leading countries as well) saw little to be gained by abandoning the par-value structure and moving to floating rates. At no time during the Truman administration did this aspect of foreign exchange-rate policy come under serious consideration either in financial circles or in the academic community.

The Later Years, 1950–52

Under the impact of the Korean War, U.S. imports rose sharply. In the first half of 1950 the surplus on goods and services was only $3 billion, and it dropped to $600 million in the second half (annual rates). For the year the surplus amounted to only $1.8 billion. This greatly eased the "dollar problem," and foreign countries were able to accumulate reserves. But in 1951 and 1952 the U.S. surplus again ran at the rate of $5 billion annually, and only by the

---

* This rate continued until August 1971, making the Japanese stabilization program one of the most successful of the entire postwar period.

continuation of large U.S. government grants and loans were the accounts balanced.

At the beginning of 1950, the U.S. objectives in foreign economic and financial policies were: (1) to contain communism and encourage the growth of democratic political and social organizations by increasing the real income of peoples in the non-Communist world; (2) to foster free convertibility of currencies based on par values and a non-discriminatory trading system; (3) to promote the economic integration of Western Europe; and (4) to pursue the Point Four program of aiding the growth of developing countries.

Point Four was launched in May 1950 when Congress approved the Act for International Development, and by the end of the year the first technical assistance agreement was negotiated with Iran. By February 1951, fifteen such agreements had been negotiated. Early in 1952 President Truman declared that Point Four would "strike at the conditions of misery that envelop half the people of the earth."

During this period the U.S. continued to firmly support the par-value system and to press for relaxation of exchange restrictions whenever the payments position of a country—such as Belgium in 1952—seemed to justify it.

More importantly, between 1950 and 1952, there was an ongoing debate, furious at times, over the use of IMF resources. Between 1946 and 1949, it had been the strongly held U.S. view that worldwide balance-of-payments difficulties and widespread exchange restrictions made it unwise for the Fund to permit broad-ranging use of its resources. Such use was, in our view, to be short-term in nature and was only to enable countries to make progress toward currency convertibility and to deal with balance-of-payments deficits. In 1948, over substantial opposition, the U.S. pushed through a decision on the operations of the Fund to the effect that countries receiving ERP assistance should not seek to use Fund resources except in highly unusual circumstances.

But by 1951 it was evident that some way should be found to "unfreeze" the IMF. At the IMF annual meeting that year, Secretary Snyder emphasized the Fund's goals and linked the short-term use of its resources to those goals; but he agreed that efforts to work out acceptable policies should be continued. Early in 1952 after long discussions by the IMF executive board, the U.S. concurred in a plan to govern use of Fund resources. In brief, it allowed virtually free use of the—ordinarily—25 percent of each country's contribution to the fund which had been made in gold (the so-called gold tranche); beyond that, more severe performance criteria were established for each country's use of IMF resources. In addition, the device of "stand-by" lines of credit was worked out. These policies have continued to guide the use of IMF resources up to the present time; agreement on them in 1952 started the Fund along the road of growing activity and influence around the world, fully justifying Secretary Snyder's firm support throughout the Fund's difficult formative years.

In 1952 the Fund also began its annual consultations with countries still maintaining restrictions on payments. At the meeting in Mexico City that year, Secretary Snyder commended that initiative (the forerunner of today's IMF "surveillance" procedures) and reiterated U.S. support of nondiscriminatory, multilateral trade and of payments free of exchange restrictions. At the long Torquay session of the GATT, late in 1950, the U.S. had used its influence to press for progress in relaxing trade restrictions. American efforts in 1951 and 1952 to create permanent administrative machinery in the GATT encountered objection from the British and others; and this was not accomplished until later. In those years of continued widespread resort to quantitative import restrictions and exchange controls,* only persistent U.S. pressure kept the nondiscriminatory trade policies alive.

Paralleling its support of the IMF, the Truman administration was active in the IBRD. During the entire period from 1947 to 1951, the Bank loaned a total of about $700 million to developing countries. Hence, loans to twelve countries totaling some $300 million in 1952 alone marked sub-

---

* Not until 1959–60 was there real progress toward currency convertibility; and the Kennedy round of trade negotiations was even later.

stantial progress in establishing the Bank as a major source of development loans. During 1951 the U.S. had begun considering the possibility of establishing an International Finance Corporation to operate in the private sector and sponsored a resolution in ECOSOC to that effect, referring the matter to the IBRD; several years later this initiative was successful.

With the advent of the Korean War, U.S. foreign policy took a new thrust. In addition to its ongoing programs of economic and technical assistance, the U.S. initiated the Mutual Defense Assistance Program; almost $6 billion was appropriated in 1950, chiefly for NATO. In succeeding years large sums were also approved to finance the Mutual Security Program. Part of the funds—$1.7 billion in fiscal 1953—was earmarked for use outside of Europe.

The administration continued to press the European countries to make progress toward economic inetgration. The Mutual Security Act of 1952 reaffirmed our previous position. During the 1952 campaign, both party platforms and both presidential candidates concurred. The U.S. continued to support the EPU which in 1951 and 1952 encountered serious payments imbalances, causing the U.S. to push the IMF into its first stand-by agreement, one with Belgium for $50 million. One visible sign of some movement toward European integration was the conclusion in 1951 (with strong U.S. support) of the treaty establishing the European Coal and Steel Community. It was ratified by six countries in June 1952 and, aside from the temporary OEEC, was the first multinational European institution.

At the end of its nearly eight years, the Truman administration could look back on a long list of major achievements in the foreign economic and financial field: the coming of age of the Bretton Woods institutions; the economic recovery of Europe and the successful monetary stabilization program in Japan; the preservation of a multilateral, non-discriminatory trade policy; a program of technical and economic assistance to developing countries; progress toward European integration; support of a par-value system with convertible currencies as the goal; and establishment of a Mutual Security Program, with strong economic aspects.

9

The View from
The Council of Economic Advisers

Leon H. Keyserling

Before examining President Truman's economic policies, let me begin by talking about the man himself. I have
never agreed with the idea that Harry Truman grew after
he got into the White House. I have not seen any president
who grows or shrinks after he gets into the White House.
He responds to new situations, and he does bigger things;
but how he does them and why he does them are determined
by the kind of man he is.

Harry Truman was shaped by conditions long before he
got to the White House. In part, these included his own
experience as what we loosely call an "average citizen," who
had his ups and downs in economic life, through no fault
of his own. That was a very important experience. Second,
President Truman's thinking was an outgrowth of the history and development of the Democratic party. There is a
straight and logical stream in the party from William Jen-
nings Bryan through Woodrow Wilson to Franklin Roosevelt and Harry Truman. Its two main elements are, first,
that the idea of watering the economic tree at the bottom,
not at the top, is not merely a political slogan but is a profound and realistic appraisal of the workings of the American
economy; second, that the responsibility of government is
different from that of business. This is not an antibusiness
sentiment; it involves a recognition that "in my father's
house there are many mansions."

Harry Truman was not against big business. If he

wanted to help small business, it was because he thought small business needed it more. Nor did Harry Truman believe it was the primary function of business to engage in public services. It may be a good thing that business in recent times has engaged in some public services, but I think Harry Truman felt that the main function of business was honorably and honestly to produce more goods and services, to try to produce them at a lower cost, and to try to translate those lower costs into lower prices. The function of protecting the public was government's responsibility. That was what Harry Truman really meant when he said there were ten thousand people in Washington representing everybody, every special interest, but he was the only one chosen to represent the people's interest and he was going to do so to the best of his ability.

Essentially this was a recognition of the function of government—a function that cannot be served by a president saying in a State of the Union message, "The government can't solve your problems; you've got to solve them in your separate and individual capacities, as 225 million citizens." Such side-stepping would be as if Roosevelt had sent emissaries to the people in bread lines in New York City to say, "Please, you tell us what to do next." That is not democracy, it is chaos; and furthermore, it is a confusion of the honorable responsibilities of government under the American system.

Harry Truman believed in a strong government. He did not believe that it should take over private enterprise; he was not a Socialist, nor was he an extreme liberal or radical (for want of a better term). But he certainly placed no limitations on the responsibility of government, something Lincoln articulated better than anyone else: "It is the function of government to do for the people what they cannot do for themselves, or cannot do so well, in their separate and individual capacities."

Those were the conditioning factors in Harry Truman's thinking about economics, along with his experiences during the Great Depression and World War II. He differed from most economists, and from the mainstream of traditional economics: most economists are steeped in the idea of scarcity, and their main function is to warn about what *cannot* be done.

There are some things that no nation is rich enough to do, and Harry Truman knew that, and he did not try to do them. But he also believed that this nation had the power to accomplish what might seem impossible. That conviction was stated first by Franklin Delano Roosevelt in his 1932 acceptance speech: "We are troubled by no plague of locusts." Roosevelt meant that there were no natural causes or intrinsic reasons why we could not do better. Under proper leadership, by invoking our own innate powers and by recognizing that the president might have to call for a very strong exercise of power, we could overcome any difficulty, no matter how great. That was certainly proved during World War II when our accomplishments exceeded the most fanciful expectations.

Before the end of World War II, I captured the phrase that seems to me typical of Harry Truman. When I wrote the essay that really led to the Employment Act of 1946, I began: "This war has awakened Americans to the promise of America." I went on to say that if we could beat our swords back into plowshares, there was nothing we could not do when we were relieved of the economic burden of using half of our national product to fight a war. Harry Truman understood that—as I will illustrate below—better than most economists, better than most people inside or outside of government. It was the basis on which he functioned.

This was Truman's Democratic tradition, augmented by his experiences during the depression: the well-being of the people is the supreme law; a country is built or rebuilt by rebuilding the people who have been destroyed; and the place to start is with the people, not by letting relief trickle down slowly to them. Let us look at the facts, at what happened, because there is no way of testing what a president does except by the results.

Let me give the results of President Truman's economic policies very simply. I will pass over 1945 and 1946 because that was a unique period of transition from war to peace. (Incidentally, it was no accident that the dire postwar prophecy by most economists of 8 million unemployed did not come to pass.) The beginning of 1947 is a fair point for me to begin because that was when both the Employment Act of 1946 and the Council of Economic Advisers became operative.

Between 1947 and 1953 the real average annual rate of economic growth was between 4.8 percent and 5 percent. Let nobody say that that was because of the stimulus of the Korean War. During the Vietnam War the real rate of economic growth averaged 2.5 percent (I'll discuss the reasons why below). Between 1947 and 1953 the unemployment rate averaged 4 percent, due in part to the difficulties of getting over the demobilization period. The trend, however, is even more important. During Harry Truman's last year in office, the unemployment rate was reduced to 2.9 percent. That sounds incredible, but even the average rate is much lower than any we have had since, if one considers a responsibly long period of time.

These figures are even more remarkable in light of the fact that the low rate of unemployment—and the downward trend of unemployment—did not result in inflation. Certainly there were inflationary periods—the figure was 10 percent when the Chinese jumped into the Korean War. Inflation was very high in 1947 too, about 7.6 percent as I recall. But the 1947 inflation was due mostly to our financing only about half of World War II out of taxation; the other half came from borrowing. During the war, the government borrowed money by selling bonds (and told people euphemistically that they were saving). After the war there was nothing left; we blew up the savings in bombs. Wars are paid for out of current products—out of current blood and out of current material. Paying off the debt of accumulated wartime bonds was an inflationary factor greater than any we have had since. These facts are not offered apologetically because, despite that 7.6 percent inflation rate in 1947, the average rate of inflation from '47 through '53 was only 3 percent; at the end of 1947 the rate was 0.8 percent. Furthermore, despite the Korean War, there was an average surplus in the federal budget during the Truman years, something that has not been achieved since.

It is an unbelievable record. Now, let us examine the reasons for that record in terms of Harry Truman and the people around him. Truman had two qualities, in perfect proportion: he supported the people he chose (unless he didn't like what they did and then he had the guts to fire them), and he recognized that he could not be an expert in many fields and therefore must rely on his specialists (but also that he had not only the right but the duty to reject their advice whenever he wanted).

One striking example of that second quality comes to mind. Truman often said that General Marshall was the greatest living American, and he almost worshipped Dean Acheson, but he flatly repudiated the advice of both of those gentlemen on the question of whether to recognize Israel. Regardless of who was right on that point, when Harry Truman wanted to, he could say no to the people he respected the most.

On the other hand, Harry Truman supported the people who worked for him. I remember once when I was in the administration, before he knew me well, I had been writing a lot of articles and the press had been making the kind of comments that they frequently make about Democratic administrations. Clark Clifford called me up and said, "You better go to see the boss."

I said to myself, "This is the end."

I went to see Truman, and he had a big green book on his desk, a scrapbook of all the things that I had written. He told me to sit down and he put his hand on the book. "Leon," he said, "I have read every damn word in this. I have read your articles. I have read what they have said about them. I have not found one word in all this criticism that says that you are not agreeing with the president of the

United States," he said. "So, let's forget about it." In other words, what I had been saying was what he believed in, and he supported his staff when he believed they were right.

Now let me say a few words about the people around President Truman. We have all heard the charge that Truman had a "crony" government. How preposterous. Certainly, he played poker with some people. I never knew who he played poker with, but I do know that the people who were generally designated as cronies (and there may have been some non-cronies in those games) never sat with the cabinet or the Security Council, wrote speeches, or attended meetings with the president. Though they were friends, these people had nothing whatsoever to do with national policy.

Another myth about Truman is that he did not have people around him of the caliber that Roosevelt had. I do not want to disparage the man who, frankly, I think was probably the greatest president we have had in modern times. Run down the lists of cabinet people and those around the two presidents: there is just no comparison. Who can compare Hull and Stettinius with Marshall and Acheson? If they really know the situation, who can compare Morgenthau with Snyder? Who can compare Dern and Swanson (the first two secretaries of war and navy) with men like Forrestal and Marshall? And if you really want to get down to it, who can compare those who are sneeringly called "the best and the brightest" with the people who, in terms of results, turned out to really be the best and the brightest? There is no one who can be compared with Charles Brannan, the greatest secretary of agriculture in the history of the Untied States. In short, we need not be defensive or embarrassed by these ignorant slurs on the Truman administration. Happily, it is constantly being reappraised more and more highly in the eyes of historians and of the people.

As the economic historian of the Truman administration (as well as the economic protagonist, for whatever reasons), I was constantly writing for publication about what was going on, why it was going on, and what we were trying to do. In this effort I had the absolute encouragement and stimulus of the president. During the years that I was on the Council of Economic Advisers, I had eight lead articles in the *New York Times Magazine*. After they appeared the president always discussed them with me the next time that I saw him alone. I have two thousand bound articles and speeches describing what was happening in that administration and why. (Ultimately these will become the property of the Truman Library.) In reviewing the record of those turbulent years, I must say that it is like trying to tear a seamless webb to separate what happened in the broad stream of Truman's economic policy between 1947 and 1950 as against '50 to '53. To examine the latter period by itself is like trying to evaluate a blossom without discussing the seeds and the fertilizer.

The first major principle that governed the economic policies of the Truman administration was that there was nothing that we as a nation could not do if we really tried. Now this is not literally true, of course. Even America could spend itself into bankruptcy or destroy its economy. But it stood to reason that if we could bear the costs of World War II, feed the world, send armies and navies and men everywhere, and actually raise the living standard of the American people more than at any time before and faster than at any time since—if we could do all that during wartime when we were blowing up half of the things our economy produced, we could do even better for the American people in peacetime.

The principle of economic growth, in accordance with our full capabilities, is not a chapter in a textbook. Growth is the very meaning of an economy: if a nation can use its resources to produce and distribute more goods and services and produce them wisely, that is the source of real wealth. Obviously, growth has to be accompanied by changes in the pattern of growth. It is strange that people who complain that growth per se would consume finite resources do not recognize that the proper management of growth is the critical factor.

Let us consider a couple of examples. Just think how much less of our resources would be consumed if instead of driving automobiles, people could use modern, swift, clean, mass transportation to get around. Or, if we transferred more of our resources from some of the things that are being built into the construction of homes. Housing is needed by every economic and social test and, without going into details, consumes far fewer resources, especially energy, than some of the competing kinds of investment that produce relatively unnecessary gadgets.

Resources, of course, have always been finite. Twenty or thirty years ago, there was an outburst of concern, and a great many books were written warning we were at the end of our resources. I never believed it. Take the 1973–74 Arab oil embargo. If Harry Truman had been president, I know he would have gotten some different advice, and I think he would have handled the crisis in a different way. I think Harry Truman might have said to the Arabs: the price is too high and we're not buying; we are not going to subject ourselves to endless years of international economic piracy; we will learn to do without your oil; we won't import it. And Truman would have set the nation on a program, an activist program, to increase the supply of energy from sources available to us.

This positive step simply was not tried in the 1970s. It would have kept us immune from price increases by the Organization of Petroleum Exporting Countries [OPEC]. I can tell you this with assurance: what the Arabs did hurt our economy—and it still does—but to imply that oil is the whole source, or even the main source, of our past or current inflation is for the birds. We have an alibi factory in Washington; what we need is a Department of Experience. The word "stagflation" was around long before the Arabs acted. The rate of inflation had slowly risen for many years to about 6 percent annually—three times what it was when we had a healthy economy, before we became the slaves of Arab oil. The current double-digit rate of inflation is due to a hundred domestic causes that we ought to be remedying and that have nothing to do with OPEC.

We ought today to combine a fair appraisal of the consequences of OPEC actions with a fair appraisal of our own shortcomings. These problems are solvable; the resource problem is solvable. Most of the talk about "non-growth," which originated with my friend John Kenneth Galbraith, came from the snobbish affluent people who had everything they wanted. They rode by the railway stations, did not like the smell, and said, "Let's change the *quality* of life, now that we've *solved* the quantity problem." This attitude implies that there is no more poverty; there are no more health-service problems; there is no more unemployment. Non-growth represents an abandonment of our commitment to full employment. It's all in *The Affluent Society* (1958).

We must consider not how well Leon Keyserling or some of the others who worked for Truman could get along if there were no growth, but what could happen to the people at large if there were no growth. Where would the jobs come from? Where would the money come from to finance the energy programs and the environmental programs that people say are more important than growth? Unless you are content to have the environmental program in conflict with the defense program, and the defense program in conflict with the educational program—in short, an economy of scarcity—the source of everything we do is economic growth.

Of course, the principle of goals, which we learned from World War II (and which all business recognizes), is the guide to performance and was fully accepted by the Truman administration. Next, having a goal means having a program that can be broken down into its components so that the relationships between investment and consumption and between business spending, consumer spending, and government spending are viable and sustainable. If there is too much business investment relative to the other demands, the result is over-capacity. If there is too little business investment, you get classic inflation (which really is not the kind we have had during the past twenty to twenty-five years).

From its inception, the Council of Economic Advisers began to build what in one of my articles I called a national prosperity budget. It was different from a federal government budget, which is really a part, or should be, of the national prosperity budget. We defined not only the ultimate goals in terms of production and employment, but what the relationships should be as well; and this entered into the recommendations we made to the president. That kind of analysis had been done during World War II. Increasingly, we recognized that it was necessary to break down the components into more parts: it was not enough to say more business investment was needed; *where* was it needed? Don't hand out tax bonanzas to businesses that are in overcapacity now and need it least; point tax reductions to encourage the production of goods that are needed the most. In other words, use tax policy selectively to bring about improvement in the distribution and balanced use of income.

I had occasion recently to testify before Senator [Russell] Long's committee, and in preparation I made a thorough study of what has happened to our tax policy since the end of World War II. Every tax program enacted during the Truman years, except the 1948 bill that he vetoed, was progressive. They all improved the redistribution of income by giving tax relief to those who needed help most, while the people who needed it least did not get too much.

One of the real accomplishments of the Truman administration was its successful nurturing of our full economic potential. And that development came long before we got into the Korean War. By looking at all the government's policies in perspective—how they affected the whole economy and how they affected these imbalances—it was possible to make full use of available resources.

During the Korean War, we simply did more of these same things, because it was a more intense and a tighter situation. *The Economics of National Defense* was issued in December 1950 as a publication of the Council of Economic

Advisers (I happen to have written it), sent to the president, and published. It presents a fairly good outline of what happened, summarized in the chapter titles. The introduction begins,

> Speed, and more speed, is imperative . . . to reach . . . maximum strength. . . . But first of all, we must define what composition of strength we strive for. There are many elements in our total strength. . . . Speed is not achieved by doing the wrong things first, nor by trying to do everything at the same time.

In "How Much of Our Resources Can We Afford for Defense?" the familiar debate was aired. The position that I always took, especially during the Korean War, was that (within some bounds, of course) the question itself was insane, because defense is not an economic program. Everybody knows that defense spending detracts from economic wealth and economic strength, but that is not why a nation does it. Economists cannot join in with the president's other advisers on decisions about what kind of weapons we need and how many. Economists have to find ways of adapting the other programs to the defense requirements.

Since the mid 1960s we have moved blatantly in the other direction. During the Vietnam War, one of the antiwar arguments was that the fighting must be stopped in order to free enough money for domestic social programs. But this did not materialize: the war was stopped (for other good reasons), and instead of expanding those social programs, we have cut back on them more and more. To try to determine international defense policy by crying wolf about the American economy is one of the most mortal blows that any thoughtful person could direct against our national interest and survival.

It is undoubtedly true that at times President Truman, with sound advice, shaped the defense program somewhat to economic considerations, but I cannot believe that President Truman would have said, "If it's going to unbalance the budget very much, we're not going to do anything about

Korea. If it's going to unbalance the budget very much, we're not going to support the creation of NATO." He knew that the budget, like all instruments of policy, is the servant and not the master of the people; the budget is an instrument and not the end purpose of the national economy.

Fortunately, although President Truman had to make some hard budget decisions, they really were not terribly hard. The American tax system is so productive that if the economy operates pretty near to full production, and pretty near full growth, there will be a budget surplus no matter what (except, of course, in a situation like World War II). It was the growth program, which Truman understood, and the economic expansion program, which he understood, that permitted him to run a budget surplus.

If, on the other hand, instead of a 5 percent growth rate, Truman had had the 2.5 percent rate that has been our average during the last twelve years, there is no way in the world (without abandoning fixed obligations under the budget or without neglecting important areas) that he could have avoided running big deficits. It is impossible to squeeze the blood of adequate revenues from the turnip of a starved economy. This was how his growth policy, his expansion policy, his economic policy, fitted in with his budget policy. And we are going into the opposite direction today.

At the beginning of the Korean War, as at the beginning of World War II, there were people who thought that the way to fight a war was to freeze everything. Just slap on price controls and wage controls with nothing else and make the people pay for fighting the war by taking less of everything else. But the expression "guns or butter" is a complete misnomer. If by "guns" we mean defense, and by "butter" we mean civilian supplies, a nation always has to have both. It is a matter of degrees. During World War II, as I have said, we had more guns *and* more butter than we had ever had before, because we made full use of that great non-secret weapon, our capacity to produce and to grow. So a very sharp debate arose. The position that prevailed, in which the growth theory was the central feature, can be summarized briefly.

First, if there was to be a cold war of indefinite duration (either after or as part of a hot war), to get the people's support, they could not be cut back too sharply. There had to be a sense of some possibility for economic progress among the American people even while a limited war was being fought.

The second point was that full production is the best cure for inflation; a stunted economy with high unemployment and a lot of idle production capacity is inflationary. Now, it is hard to realize what a revolutionary idea that was at the time. It faces just as much of a battle for acceptance today, however, because economists are still reading in the old textbooks that if you have ten apples and there are eleven buyers, the price will go up, and if there are nine buyers, the price will go down: "supply and demand." Actually, if I control the supply of the apples and I want to cover my costs and make a predetermined profit, I will charge more per apple when I sell nine than when I sell eleven. (This, incidentally, is not an imaginary scenario; this is a behavior pattern. I do not say that critically, I am merely an objective observer. This is the behavior pattern of the administered sectors of American industry. They raise their prices faster when they sell much less than the full potential. I could cite a hundred examples.)

When the effort to fight inflation is focused on cutting back production and thus curtailing employment opportunity, the result is tremendous scarcities in selective parts of the economy, which are highly inflationary. The biggest areas of inflation now are in housing, medical costs, food, and energy. I have been pointing out for twenty-five years that, contrary to the story of the apples, there has been the greatest inflation when there was stagnation and recession, and the least with full employment. (By full employment I do not mean just manpower and woman-power and teenage-power, I mean brains, skills, business inventiveness, plant, everything that makes up an economy, going full-steam.)

The last time we had the kind of price performance that I am talking about—inflation getting down to 0.8 percent—was under the Truman administration when we had those crucial components of economic expansion. Then "King Arthur" [Burns] came in for eight years: first he was chairman of the Council of Economic Advisers, where he influenced both fiscal and monetary policy; then he appointed [Raymond] Saulnier as his successor, and they shared the same philosophy. Burns was terribly worried that 0.8 percent inflation was too high, and that 2.8 percent unemployment was too low. So, without detailing all of the tightening-up that went on over the period, the Eisenhower administration succeeded from 1953 to 1961 in raising unemployment from 2.9 to 7.6 percent. But when they left office the rate of inflation was two and a half times what it was when they started.

Then Walter Heller became CEA chairman. Under Kennedy and Johnson, economic policy was mainly a facsimile of what the Truman administration had done. They debated the question of inflation and growth, and they plumped for growth; by 1966 the unemployment rate was down. Then some bad things happened that I won't get into. (Basically, they did not want to raise taxes at the height of the Vietnam War.) Anyway, when they were doing well, the Democrats reduced unemployment from 7.6 in 1961 to 3.8 in 1966. And starting in 1961 with 7.6 inflation, the Democrats averaged for six years 1.5 percent annual inflation. And they had a real average annual economic growth of 5 percent.

Did succeeding administrations learn anything from this? Absolutely not. We have gone amiss now for far more than a decade. Every time it has been tried, it has been proven that you do not stop inflation by cutting the production of goods and services. Every time it has been tried, inflation has worsened. At the depth of the recession of '73–'74, which was the greatest downturn since the Great Depression, we had the highest rate of inflation since the Civil War. In the first quarter 1979, with a real economic growth rate deliberately cut back to an annual rate of 0.7 percent, inflation was 13 percent.

The Carter administration is still trying to conquer inflation by cutting the growth rate, by deliberately running unemployment upward, and by running plant capacity deliberately downward. In that way they think they are going to cure inflation.

The Truman administration emphatically rejected this kind of fake cure for inflation. Although controls were needed and were necessary at that time, by the end of '52 and early '53 we had arrived at a situation where even with the rapid diminution of controls and their eventual abandonment, prices remained stable for a considerable period of years. The reason for that success was the economic environment created earlier when the output of goods and services and the benefits of high growth and low unemployment had been fostered.

Truman was a great believer in the fact that a major facet of fighting inflation could not and should not be done by the government. In the Truman administration, when we talked about planning, we did not talk about planning the economy, we talked about planning what the government did. We said that the government itself should not fly blind. We were never caught in a situation that has recurred repeatedly in recent years, where the government argues that Federal Reserve should be hitched up to one side of the economic cart and tax policy should be hitched up to the other side, so that one could balance the difficulties of the other.

Truman greatly encouraged opening government up to the public. One example was the working relationships of the Council of Economic Advisers. We had a labor advisory group—although we had to hold separate meetings with the AFL and the CIO. They did not break with us (although they did break with the Kennedy administration, for whatever reasons). Years later they said that they had had the most profitable relations with the CEA during the Truman years. The council also had relationships with the National

Farmers' Union and with other farm groups, but more importantly we tried to build relations with the business community. That is a hard thing for a Democratic administration to do.

When I became chairman of the council, I was asked, "How about taking over the Department of Commerce advisory body as the CEA business advisory group?"

I said, "We can't advise with a hundred or two hundred people, and I have no desire to go down to Greenbrier [a West Virginia resort] to play softball. Let me choose twelve people from that group." It just so happened that three of the twelve later became secretaries in Eisenhower's cabinet: George Humphrey of Consolidated Coal, Marion Folsom of Eastman Kodak, and Charlie Wilson of General Motors. Others in the CEA business advisory group included the heads of major corporations—General Foods, Sears, International Harvester, Armstrong Cork, etc. We met formally many times a year and supplemented those meetings by my traveling with A. D. Whiteside, the head of Dun and Bradstreet. We had off-the-record meetings with the top business leaders in all of the big cities (that's the only way I could ever get in to the Duquesne Club in Pittsburgh, likewise the Union League Club in New York). And the general reaction was, "Well, before these meetings we had some strange views about you people, but now we look at it differently." And a number of them wrote letters to Averell Harriman to that effect.

Truman also encouraged the promotion of good working relationships within the departments of government. I have heard stories about how the Truman cabinet was divided into two groups, the conservatives and the liberals. That was true to a degree, but it was not the controlling factor in most matters. In the council we grouped our staff into major elements of policy: fiscal policy, cyclical policy, stabilization policy, wage-price policy, investment policy, economic outlook, etc. Then we developed their counterparts throughout the government by setting up interdepartmental staff committees, usually under the chairmanship of a member of the council staff operating in that field. Thus we achieved a parallel organization on a broader basis. As for preparing the draft of the Economic Report, we did two a year. (They have never been able to do more than one since, with three times as many staff.) As soon as one draft report was completed, we started on the next one. We also began making so-called economic assumptions which went to the Budget Bureau, and there was a most harmonious relationship between those economic assumptions—including the policy of growth—and what turned up in the president's budget, with give and take on all sides.

For example, after all the discussions had taken place at lower levels, John Snyder would have his copy of the draft of the Economic Report long before we discussed it with the president. He and I would talk on the phone, and in three or four minutes any dispute was usually settled. There were usually no jarring disagreements to be resolved by the president; there was a commonality of purpose, and a president who led us that way. I could say the same thing about other members of the cabinet.

I think that it would be well for students of the Truman administration to read the available sources on the history of that administration—there are a lot of them—and try to wake up their fellow citizens to the lessons they can learn.

Every single problem we face today existed during the Truman years—to be sure with some alterations. Why can't the present leaders begin to learn from the great experience of the American economy instead of taking steps diametrically opposite to the ones that succeeded? I say this not merely out of admiration for what President Truman did, with help from all of us, but out of concern as an American about the future of our country. We have lost that greatest of all gifts, the gift to open our minds and to learn.

10

The Employment Act of 1946

James L. Sundquist, Bertram R. Gross,
Leon H. Keyserling, and Walter S. Salant

Editor's Note: As early as January 1942 the National Resources Planning Board had declared that "a positive program of postwar economic expansion and full employment, boldly conceived and vigorously pursued, is imperative." In January 1944, President Roosevelt proclaimed "the right to a useful and remunerative job" as the first of a new economic bill of rights. His Republican opponent in that year's election, Thomas E. Dewey, echoed this with the pronouncement that "if at any time there are not sufficient jobs in private employment to go around, the government can and must create job opportunities, because there must be jobs for all in this country."

Legislation to translate this idea into law was first introduced in the Senate in January 1945 (S.380, the Murray-Wagner bill). It was this bill, somewhat reworded, which President Truman urged Congress, in his message of September 6, 1945, to enact without delay. However, opposition in the House of Representatives forced postponement of final action and also led to considerable compromises. As finally signed into law by President Truman on February 20, 1946, the law bore the title "Employment Act of 1946" and opened with this declaration of policy:

> The congress hereby declares that it is the continuing policy and responsibility of the Federal Government to use all practicable means consistent with its needs and obligations and other essential considerations of national

policy, with the assistance and cooperation of industry, agriculture, labor, and state and local governments, to coordinate and utilize all its plans, functions and resources

(1) For the purpose of creating and maintaining, in a manner calculated to foster and promote free competitive enterprise and the general welfare, conditions under which there will be afforded useful employment opportunities, including self-employment, for those able, willing and seeking to work, and

(2) To promote maximum employment, production and purchasing power.

The bill required the president to submit annually an Economic Report, setting forth current levels of employment, production, and purchasing power, together with the levels needed to effectuate the conditions set forth in the policy declaration and a program for carrying out that policy. The bill created a three-member Council of Economic Advisers to assist the president and a Joint Committee on the Economic Report to consider and report on it.

James L. Sundquist

The most important decision of the early period of the Truman administration concerning domestic economic policy was the decision made in 1946 that from that point on it would be the responsibility of the United States government to manage (maybe that is too strong a word—to manipulate, to steer, to guide, to influence, to control) the economy in order to get the maximum benefits and results. This was truly a revolutionary step in the country's history.

There is a wistful little passage in Herbert Hoover's memoirs in which he said, in effect, "There have been a lot of depressions previously in the country—Van Buren had one, Grant had one, Cleveland had one; nothing happened to them. Why did the roof fall in on me?"

This was quite true. Before 1946, the president of the United States was not required to have an economic policy; and most of them—including Van Buren, Cleveland, and Grant (and Hoover might have mentioned Harding as well)—who presided over the government in times of deep depression did not have a policy. It is really astonishing to look back at Van Buren's State of the Union message in 1837, or Grant's in 1873, or Cleveland's in 1893, and find that although the country was economically depressed, the subject was not even mentioned. A depression was something happening over there, in the private sector, that had nothing to do with the federal government.

But since 1946 every president has had to have an economic policy that is announced at least once a year. This has marked a profound change in the role of the United States government and in its relation to the economy, in its relation to economic life, and in the nature of the presidency itself.

To digress for a moment, it is interesting to note that this great addition to the responsibilities of the president was initiated on Capitol Hill. Harry Truman eventually endorsed the proposition, but I do not think it was ever very high on his list of priorities. The move was not initiated by the president trying to expand the duties of his office. When Congress first considered the early drafts of what became the Employment Act of 1946, the forerunner of the Council of Economic Advisers was located in the legislative branch; and it was Congress that was going to formulate and enact the country's economic policies. That provision disappeared very early in the evolution of the bill: it quickly became clear that this duty was one for the president of the United States.

Comparing the postwar period to the present, one is struck by the sense of confidence then that full employment could indeed be achieved. Leon Keyserling, Bertram Gross, Gerhard Colm—these people did not have the slightest doubt that if they could define the condition of the economy, they would know what to do about it. This certainty stands in sharp contrast to the people around Jimmy Carter who are possessed by the gravest doubts that it is within the capacity of the federal government to direct and influence the economy in a favorable way.

The new breed of economists during the Truman administration figured that if the problem was defined and the course was clear, it was perfectly within the power of government to set things aright. Economic policy would be based on economic analysis rather than on moral dogmas or received wisdom, as in the twenties. Nor would it be based, as in the thirties, on frank experimentation without benefit of either a plan or a theory.

Policymakers, incidentally, did not necessarily have as much confidence in this group of economists as the economists had in themselves. Washington was still full of pre-Keynesians who never quite got converted, who still thought of economic policy in moral terms. I think that Harry Truman basically was one of those. He had trouble blending the advice of the new economists with the advice he was getting from the businessmen, the bankers, and the lawyers who previously had been accustomed to making economic policy. The new economists, self-assured and full of zeal, had to fight their way into the confidence of the president. But the authors of the Employment Act of 1946 had engineered a brilliant way of bringing this about. With the creation of the Council of Economic Advisers, a group of these economists was at the president's elbow at all times. The law required him to sign an annual report that would be prepared by the council, giving them an unparalleled opportunity to influence him, to guide his policy, and basically to educate him. He had to submit to their education.

The story of economic policy over the next twenty years was that the education took. By the time of the Kennedy and Johnson administrations, the Keynesian economists had pretty complete mastery and control of the nation's economic policy. But the crucial first step was taken in this yeasty period, this time of great confidence, Truman's first couple of years.

The Employment Act of 1946

BERTRAM R. GROSS

In talking about the Employment Act of 1946 historians are going to miss an awful lot unless they examine the concept behind that law. There are many things I could add to Steven Bailey's book on the subject (*Congress Makes a Law: The Story behind the Employment Act of 1946* [New York: Columbia University Press, 1950]). There was a bill which was proposed to Sen. James Murray (D-Mont.) by the National Farmers Union [NFU] during the course of the 1944 campaign. Like Jim Patton and Russell Smith of the NFU, who worked with Murray at that time, and Louis Bean of the Department of Agriculture, who was consulting with them both on the formulation of policy, many of us in the administration were a little concerned about the easy campaign rhetoric of promising jobs for all. President Roosevelt, of course, had enunciated the idea of an economic bill of rights earlier in the year. Dewey was backed into the position where he also had to use the dirty words "and jobs for all"; but there was growing concern that this was merely a political promise and we would not see serious performance.

The bill that the National Farmers Union submitted to Senator Murray was a strictly Keynesian proposal. Personally, I did not like it, but I thought it was a marvelous way to begin a discussion of doing *something*. If I recall—and I think Bailey has the details in *Congress Makes a Law*—it was a bill to guarantee a $20 billion federal investment in order to stabilize the level of employment.

As soon as the proposal came in, my role was to say, "Let's send this immediately to every department and, of course, to the Budget Bureau for comment." Thus, there soon accumulated in my office a long series of very interesting memoranda discussing the National Farmers Union proposal. The NFU, speaking in strictly Keynesian terms, had started a discussion. I recommend that historians and others who are trying to understand that period, go back to the full set of reports. They were published by our committee [the Senate Committee on Banking and Currency].

The reports reveal some very interesting discussions. There were those who objected to an "undue" emphasis on investment: the basic theme of the proposal was that the instability of private investment necessitated—to use a Keynesian term—government socialization of the investment function in order to stabilize the economy. Some in the Labor Department wanted greater attention paid to consumption. There were big debates on that. I remember getting the two sides together and saying, "Well, if some of you are so strong for investment and some for consumption, what about adding them up? And for a change, let's just look at the total level of GNP as the way we measure what is happening."

There were also some who felt that the only approach to the postwar period was to bust up the trusts and other large-scale combinations; on the other hand, there were those who felt we should continue centralized wartime planning. The more realistic people in all the various departments felt that you could not go very far with the anti-trust approach, even if it were desirable, and that the continuation of central planning in wartime terms was impossible— whether desirable or not.

The original version of the full employment bill brought all of these ideas together. It placed heavy emphasis on government spending, for any purposes whatsoever, as a last resort to see to it, first, that the country did not have a depression and, second, that the right to employment was federally protected. In the bill's early versions, we probably put so much emphasis on the last-resort aspect that we did not give enough attention to all of the other policies at the disposal of the federal government. This was corrected as the drafts of the bill were refined.

I do not agree at all with Leon Keyserling's acceptance of the ultraconservative critique that the original bill proposed straight down-the-line spending; it did not. But the protective array of other positive measures was not well spelled out in either the original committee print (December 1944) or the January 1945 version. When the Murray-

Truman bill was finally introduced in the Senate, it had the support of the four leading committee chairmen and four liberal Republicans (whom we were able to dig up through great effort): Wayne Morse (Ore.), George Aiken (Vt.), Charles Tobey (N.H.), and William Langer (N.D.).

The Senate version, reported first out of a subcommittee and then out of the full Banking and Currency Committee, did not provide for congressional domination; it was based clearly on the principle of presidential initiative. Those of us who worked on this version did not think that this principle should be blurred by prescribing specific administrative instrumentalities in the office of the president. This was one of the strategic political decisions made by Senators Murray, Robert F. Wagner (D-N.Y.), Joseph O'Mahoney (D-Wyo.), and the other supporters of the original legislation. Since we were immediately subjected to unfair attack on two fronts—one, that our only concern was compensatory spending, whether for investment or consumption, and the other, that we were being national economic planners (which we were in a mild sense)—we down-played the specific measures that the president might use.

There was also a good bureaucratic reason for doing this: the Treasury had its ideas, and the Budget Bureau had its ideas. I remember that eminent student of public administration, Luther Gulick, pulling me aside and saying, "Don't be confused between the Bureau of the Budget and the national economic budget. Don't ever put the Budget Bureau in charge of this kind of thing." But our position was not even to discuss it; instead, we tried to get the opposition to propose the administrative instrumentalities. It made them look constructive while, in fact, they were trying to undermine the policy.

Actually, it was Sen. Robert A. Taft (R-Ohio) who offered the first administrative proposal: a director of the national economic budget who would serve as an assistant to the president. Taft accepted the principle of presidential initiative. He was smart enough, or dedicated enough, to avoid all the trendy schemes for an economic supreme court or some kind of board made up of people from all around the country, the Congress, and the White House, working together to formulate economic policies. It was not until the real dirty work on policy came to fruition in the House of Representatives that the conservative coalition proposed a broad, inchoate body. Only our insistence on presidential initiative prevented creation of an independent council of economic advisers and produced instead a Council of Economic Advisers to the President.

Although we were all tacit "growth-men" in that period, the transition from thinking and talking about economic stability to acceptance of the fully mature concept of growth and expansion was tied up with the development of the Economic Expansion Act of 1949 (which Brent Spence introduced as chairman of the House Banking and Currency Committee). It provided the legislative basis for the kind of last-resort intervention by the government in any area of the economy that was in basic short supply, such as steel.

You might call the Economic Expansion Act a minor stepping stone between the Employment Act and the recent Humphrey-Hawkins bill for full employment and balanced growth. The Economic Expansion Act of 1949 was necessary because it went beyond the Employment Act and articulated not only a general policy of expansion, but a whole specific set of backup measures. For all sorts of reasons that legislation did not move, but it was the intra-agency consideration of it that I regard, in retrospect, as crucial. It provided a way of articulating throughout the government's economic and political establishment the concepts of economic growth which were then being developed.

Leon H. Keyserling

It is a fallacy to think that John Maynard Keynes had anything of substance to do with the idea behind the Employment Act of 1946 or with the policies of the Truman administration. John Maynard Keynes lived at a time of worldwide depression and dealt admirably with the problems of his period. No economist can deal with the problems of a future time.

John Maynard Keynes's idea, as it is understood by Americans, was based almost solely on what is called compensatory spending: that is, when business is slow, government should spend more money to take up the slack. This is done by borrowing and using the money for public improvement. It is a valuable idea, but it was not the idea underlying the Employment Act and it certainly was not the idea underlying the administration of President Truman. The economic policy of the Truman years grew basically not out of Keynesian economics, but out of the New Deal experience with what the federal government could do. Incidentally, although Keynes is often given credit for the early public-works spending of the New Deal, his great book which first attracted widespread attention [*The General Theory of Employment, Interest and Money*] did not come out until 1936. The first three or four years of the New Deal were entirely independent of anything Keynes said or did. The New Deal was indigenous to America and so were the Truman policies. They were based primarily on our experiences before and during World War II, which taught us how much we could accomplish if we did our best. The Truman policies were based on the concept of growth which John Kenneth Galbraith said in the *New York Times* I had grafted on to Keynesian economics. But Keynes's was a static concept and the Truman policies were not. They were indigenous to the nature of Harry S. Truman, and they meshed with the advice he received from many important sources within his own administration.

Compensatory spending (as we understand it à la Keynes) was never tried during the Truman administration; it was never needed. The compensatory-spending policy was a hallmark of the first two or three years of the New Deal: PWA, WPA, CWA, etc. That policy had been embodied in bills introduced again and again by Senators Wagner, Edward P. Costigan (D-Colo.), and Robert M. La Follette (D-Wisc.), going back to 1929—and I was *there*. I was there in 1933 when the first $3.3 billion public-works appropriation got into the National Recovery Administration [NRA], over the opposition of President Roosevelt—and if you do not believe that, read the recent competent biography of the secretary of labor by George Martin, *Madam Secretary: Frances Perkins* [Boston: Houghton Mifflin, 1976]. Compensatory spending was a concept lifted out of Senator Wagner's files on the basis of bills that had been introduced since 1929 —and certainly *then* Keynes was not an influence—based on studies made by Leo Wolman at Columbia and by others.

There have always been discussions of full employment, but there was no discussion of anything resembling the Employment Act of 1946 before early 1944, when the Pabst Brewing Company conducted an essay contest on postwar full employment. (There were some thirty-seven thousand entrants.) I wrote a very simple essay at that time, called "The American Economic Goal." It is almost an exact model of the act as it became law (after going through various committee versions), with a single exception. I suggested a composite committee, reflecting my interest in the parliamentary system, whereas ultimately the primary economic initiative was entrusted to the president.

After the Pabst essay, I was called to New York to help Senator Wagner in his 1944 reelection campaign. I had known Bert Gross for many years and had (and still have) tremendous respect for his abilities. (He is, among other things, a wonderful writer.) I invited him to New York to help write speeches for the Wagner campaign because I was so busy with the war housing program. It was during this time that I discussed with him—and he certainly was very receptive—an employment bill that closely resembled the broad plenary statute that I had outlined in the Pabst essay.

The next step was, as I recall it (Jim Patton got into the picture, of course), that a committee was set up, composed of Bertram Gross, Edward F. Prichard, Jr., and myself, to draft the act. I subquently dropped out because of my preoccupation with war housing. They drafted something that politically had absolutely no chance of passage in the Congress; furthermore, the proposal was fundamentally wrong. After stating all the curlicues and all the exceptions, it was a bill to use additional government spending to remedy deficiencies in employment and production.

I felt that this approach was wrong because other policies were equally involved—monetary policy, social security policy, farm policy, housing policy, every policy. I thought we needed a unified national economic program, and the bill as it finally emerged left the way free to devise a coordinated strategy. I think that that was a wise decision.

WALTER S. SALANT

One main conceptual contribution of the Council of Economic Advisers, under the influence of Leon Keyserling, was to implant in government policy the ideas, first, that the economic performance to be expected, or demanded, was full use of our potential and, second, that economic growth was possible because the labor force was growing and because productivity was constantly increasing (or so we used to think; we have some doubts about that now).

In the 1940s, in academic professional writings, there was beginning to be some interest in the theory of growth. But it was still new even when it was introduced as an important aspect of government policy. Unquestionably, it was mainly through Leon Keyserling's influence that a concept of growth was substituted for the notion of merely cyclical fluctuations. I have discussed this in my article, "The Intellectual Contributions of the Council of Economic Advisers," in *History of Political Economy* [5:36–49].

I do have a minor disagreement with Keyserling's statement that Keynes had nothing to do with the Employment Act. That is true in a certain sense; but what I think needs to be emphasized is, first, that the intellectual climate of the time was greatly influenced by Keynes's book, *The General Theory of Employment, Interest and Money,* and, second, that the burden of that book is not compensatory spending in the case of cyclical fluctuations. This is not a book about policy, it is a book about theory; and the question that it was written to answer was what determines the level of aggregate output and employment.

The reason Keynes's book was important has to do with something that applies to all spheres of intellectual endeavor: when facts and theory begin to disagree, not much happens to the older and increasingly outdated theory. All through the thirties, every proposal for the kind of thing that Keynes was advocating was rejected by most professional economists on theoretical grounds to which nobody had a good rejoinder. What Keynes's book did was provide a theoretical answer of what determines output, something that had hitherto not been available. There were plenty of people who advocated spending before the appearance of that book, but they did not really become accepted because they lacked theoretical arguments.

I am citing this as a specific example of a generalization made, I think, by James Conant: "It takes no collection of facts to displace a theory; it takes a theory to kill a theory." This was Keynes's contribution; and he was a major factor in the intellectual environment of the time, even though he had nothing directly to do with the 1946 Employment Act.

As Bertram Gross has pointed out, compared to the pre–World War II era, we have had great success in avoiding serious and prolonged depressions. The question is, could we get out of our present economic difficulties by adopting policies like those of the Truman administration?

I think that the difficulties we are having today are new; they have not occurred before. We have had periods of inflation before, and periods of decline and of much-less-than-full employment, but we never had a period when declining demand, employment, and output were accompanied by a continued rise in prices. In part, I think the present administration's difficulties are not a result of the incompetence of its economic advisers, but of an intellectual problem that has not yet been resolved.

But that is only part of the problem. It has been greatly accentuated by the administration's self-inflicted wounds, of which there have been quite a few; these have made things worse. But I am not sure that I have detected anything in our past economic experiences that would contribute to the resolution of today's problems. Indeed, our success in resolving past problems may contribute to the lack of solutions today. What I mean is that the experiences of the fifties and the sixties have led people to expect that real income is going to continually rise, that in periods of expansion prices may go up, and in periods of contraction they will come down. But now, even though the economy is contracting, prices seem not to be going down—perhaps because of our expectations. In my view, this is only one example of the fact that the solution of some problems tends, in turn, to create new ones. That, I think, is part of what we are suffering from today.

11

Comments

W. Averell Harriman, Thomas C. Blaisdell, Jr., James E. Webb, Elmer B. Staats, Henry H. Fowler, David H. Stowe, and Bertram R. Gross

W. Averell Harriman

The international economic situation when I came home from Moscow was grave indeed: there was what we used to call a "dollar shortage." I had first recommended to President Roosevelt that we give due consideration to the economic problems of Europe. In a telegram from Moscow —I think it was in February 1945—before the end of the war, I indicated that I was convinced that the Western European countries would be in a very difficult postwar position not because of the destruction of the war, but because of both the complete dislocation that had occurred and the lack of any reserves with which to get their economies going again. I was concerned that Stalin would not only take over the Eastern European countries, but would reach out and find in Western Europe a situation that would further his plans for the worldwide expansion of communism.

There was a great demand to bring the American boys home, and we rapidly liquidated our military force. General Marshall was under tremendous pressure: everyone wanted their sons, husbands, sweethearts, and brothers to return home at once. We instituted a plan to bring the men home according to the number of months they had served abroad. The practical military effect was to destroy each and every unit abroad.

I knew this when I came home from Moscow. Secretary

[of State James F.] Byrnes let me come by way of the Far East so I could talk to Chiang Kai-shek and General Marshall in China and then to General [Douglas] MacArthur. I wanted to tell MacArthur to be careful, to warn him that he was going to have difficulties with the Soviet Union in Japan. One forgets now that Stalin wanted Hokkaido Island as his zone of occupation in Japan—I knew that; he told me so.

On that trip home I learned what a disaster this method of demobilization was. Our plane had a long flight from Moscow and needed repairs, but we couldn't find a single base that had all the necessary mechanics and maintenance personnel. It was not until we got to Hawaii that we found a complete unit.

I was asked by Jimmy Byrnes in March 1946 to go to London as ambassador; and when President Truman told me how serious he considered the world situation to be, I went. I knew the British situation well. I had been part of the group that had insisted that the British end their exports and devote all of their production capacity to the war. I knew it would take a good deal of time and money after the war to reestablish Britain's export trade, and I was very anxious, therefore, to have Lend-Lease extended. In fact, when Oliver Littleton, the minister of supply, came over here, I recommended that he discuss this with President Roosevelt so that there could be an understanding. Littleton's reply, whether he got it from Churchill or not, was, "Well, let's wait until the end of the war; you're our good friends." So nothing was done.

I do not think anyone in America realized what a sacrifice the British had made for our common good in abandoning their exports. They would never have been in as bad a postwar position as they were if they had maintained their exports. They were extraordinarily good allies during the war and did everything they could to carry their share. I knew that the rest of Europe would be in difficulty, and I was certain that Stalin would attempt to use the Communist parties to dominate Europe.

The mistake people made was to think that Stalin would

move with the Red Army. In fact, his intention was to use the strength of both the Maquis in France, who were largely controlled by the Communists, and the Communist-led Italian resistance movement. Stalin expected that those two countries would be taken over by the Communists, following electoral victories. Of course, he was wrong, but I am utterly certain that if it had not been for President Truman's extraordinary readiness to add to his domestic problems those of the rest of the world, Stalin would have taken over Western Europe.

Now, in spite of the fact that at home there was a shortage of beef and the prices were high, we continued to send grain to feed Europe. Clinton Anderson was the secretary of agriculture, and I made it my business to get very close to him and to understand his problems. He naturally wanted to help increase food production, and that meant feeding more animals. I took him abroad in 1947 to see firsthand what had happened in Europe. He then joined in a report endorsing the policy of taking grain away from our animals and sending it to feed the people of Western Europe. For this, I think he deserves a great deal of credit. Anderson gave this policy his enthusiastic support, and he took a lot of criticism of his position from agriculture in this country. Coming as he did from a ranch state, it was a very courageous act indeed. The winter of 1947–48 in Europe was terrible; there was an almost total lack of coal; there was hunger and cold. We sent over what was called interim aid, which really saved Europe.

The European nations had no dollars to buy anything. British credit helped a little, but it was not enough, and they needed much more; France was in desperate shape, and so was Italy. In spite of the president's problems here at home, he supported one of the most extraordinarily generous and understanding acts. Of course, I thought it was also an intelligent act of self-interest because if Western Europe had fallen into the hands of Stalin, we would have lost all our war gains: we would have had another dictator at the Atlantic. The ERP was an amazingly wise program and policy.

It was already well under way when I came home from Great Britain and joined it as chairman of the committee. (Nicknamed the Harriman Committee, its proper title was the Economic Recovery Committee.)

I knew that our aid to Europe made the administration's problems at home very much more difficult. The fact that the economy was controlled as skillfully as it was is a great credit to Mr. Truman and his advisers. My own feeling is that we perhaps could have done a little bit more by using higher interest rates, but that would not have protected the value of the American bond market—and President Truman had a firm personal belief that the value of our government bonds should not falter.

Thomas C. Blaisdell, Jr.

One of the greatest privileges of my life was working with Averell Harriman in the Department of Commerce when I came back from Europe. Little is known of the work done by that Harriman Committee, and particularly the technical job done by Dick Bissell, who put together the materials used to sell the Marshall Plan in Congress.

I will never forget Bissell going to testify. He took to the Congress a huge stack of computations showing the economics of the Marshall Plan. Every country had to get this, that, or the other, and this information eventually had to be matched up with the relief work being done in Europe. It was the amazing, imaginative, creative work of this group of technicians that laid the technical groundwork for the Marshall Plan in terms of operations.

I want to say a little more about the problems that Governor Harriman faced in London. I call this period in international trade the period of semibarter. So much of the postwar activity was carried out between governments that the fundamental economic problem was how to get back to some kind of private international trade. The establishment of the International Monetary Fund, the International Bank, and the International Trade Organization (which failed) was all oriented toward the smooth functioning of private enterprise in the international field. But that situation did not exist at the end of the war. The net result was that none of these organizations, foreseen and put together at Bretton Woods, performed their anticipated functions until considerably later. Other economic machinery had to be found in the interim.

This was effectively done only because U.S. grain allocations staved off starvation in Western Europe during 1946 and 1947. As Governor Harriman noted, much of the work in this area was done by the Department of Agriculture. These activities have received only a cursory examination and need to be looked at much more carefully by historians working on this period.

Another rather remarkable episode was President Truman's request to former President Hoover to shed some light on the bitter controversy going on in Washington over what American economic policy toward a defeated Germany should be. The question was, "What should be the limits on German economic development?" Some said that Germany was an important part of the European economy, that we could not hold that country down for long. Others said that Germany must never be allowed to regain its economic strength.

In the face of that dispute, President Truman asked Herbert Hoover to go to Europe and put the presidential plane at his disposal. Hoover had been the great benefactor of Europe following World War I—his reputation was certainly made there—and it was expected that he would be very helpful. Unfortunately, Hoover's report to the president was limited to the specific question he had been asked to explore, that of Germany, and did not reach the larger question of Western Europe. This shortcoming, I think, delayed consideration of the boarder European problems: they were clearly present but were not understood in the United States.

Governor Harriman has mentioned how slow we were to realize the extent of demoralization in Europe as a result of the war. It was not simply physical destruction. There was plenty of that wherever you went in Germany, Britain, and France, but more important was the destruction of the whole economic life. Corporations had been broken up; commercial firms had been disrupted; trade had been destroyed. For trading, we had substituted government allocation of goods and services of all kinds. This was something we did not comprehend at all in the United States, and the administration itself was slow to really grasp what was involved.

Let me cite just one example. While Governor Harriman was ambassador in London immediately after the war, Will Clayton, the undersecretary of state for economic affairs, came to Europe. He was working on the structure of the proposed International Trade Organization. (This was eventually turned down by the Congress.) Clayton sat in my office in London and telephoned Washington to tell them he was returning the next day. The question of what was to happen to Lend-Lease was under discussion in Washington. After the phone call he turned to me and said, "I think we are in good shape because they are not going to make any decision on Lend-Lease until I get home." We were more than a little surprised the next morning to read in the *Times* that President Truman had signed the recommendation terminating Lend-Lease immediately.

This was a slap in the face, both to our representation in London and to the British and the Soviet governments. Of course, the protests immediately hit Washington, and the decision was reversed. Ships which had been turned around and started home were turned around again to go back and complete their missions. I cite this simply as an illustration of how the situation in Europe was misunderstood. Theodore White's *Fire in the Ashes: Europe in Mid-Century* (1953) is, I think, the most dramatic and probably most honest account of the period.

Let me now turn to another incident. For political

reasons, the machinery in Europe that would administer the Marshall Plan had to be negotiated with each of the participant governments; this meant that there was a different set of problems to be solved every time. But the real difficulty, which Harriman had seen so clearly, was that to be effective, the Marshall Plan had to be run as a European, rather than country-by-country, operation.

The establishment of the European machinery was slow, and the effective part of it—the most effective part, in my judgment—was not only the use of Marshall funds to ship materials, but the establishment of another functioning financial center, the European Payments Union.

The EPU was sort of a cross between a government treasury and a federal reserve system. Through it, trade in Europe had a clearance center; European business people could get their loans and make their clearing of assets and liabilities there. The EPU meant, in short, the reestablishment of real trade.

Interestingly enough, the European Payments Union is being largely reestablished today in the proposals, now offered by France and Germany, for a new European unit of trade. I am not sure what they are going to call this unit of trade, but it becomes the direct competitor to the dollar in some of the international functions which are to be carried on. The steps now being taken in Europe follow in very considerable part the activities of the European Payments Union.

James E. Webb

It is important to recognize the economic difficulties we faced at the end of the war: inflation and handling the public debt. Let me quote from President Truman's budget message for 1949:

> The expenditures of the Federal Government are still inescapably dominated by the war and its aftermath.

In the fiscal year 1949, 79 percent of our expenditures directly reflect the cost of war, the effects of war and our efforts to prevent a future war: National Defense—International Affairs—Veterans' Benefits—Interest on the Public Debt—Tax Refunds. This should be a sobering thought to all of us as we strive for the creation of lasting peace among the nations of the world. Only 21 percent of our expenditures financed the Government's programs in the broad areas of: Social Welfare—Housing—Education—Research—Agriculture—Natural Resources — Transportation — Finance — Commerce — Industry—Labor—General Administration.

Noting that for the current fiscal year, 1948, the revised estimates indicated expenditures of $37.7 billion and receipts of $45.2 billion, Truman announced a surplus of $7.5 billion "which should be used to reduce the public debt."

On the subject of aid to Europe, the president said:

The budgetary implications of failure to achieve recovery in Europe and other crucial areas deserve additional emphasis. Should failure of these programs result in a further extension of totalitarian rule, we would have to reexamine our security position and take whatever steps might be necessary under the circumstances. The costs of added military strength, if Europe should succumb to totalitarian rule, would far exceed the costs of the program of economic aid now before the Congress.

Clearly the Communist threat was the rationale for his decisions concerning postwar economic recovery.

Turning to the public debt, he said:

The question of taxation must be considered in the framework of the budgetary program and the danger of further inflation. One of our most effective weapons in fighting inflation is a substantial budget surplus for reduction of the national debt. If we make this protection less effective we shall have to rely much more heavily on direct price, wage, and rationing controls which we all agree should be held to a minimum.

As of June 30, 1947, the public debt was $258 billion. Mr.

Truman predicted that budget surpluses of over $7 billion for fiscal year 1948 and nearly $5 billion for fiscal year 1949 would permit further reduction of the public debt, leaving it at $246 billion by June 30, 1949.

In his 1950 budget message the president said:

> This is the fourth budget prepared since the close of World War II. The character of the postwar world still presents many complex problems and unanswered questions. This budget is the clearest expression that can be given at this time to the program which the Government of the United States should follow in the world today.
>
> It is founded on a conviction that the United States must continue to exert strong, positive efforts to achieve peace in the world and grow in prosperity at home. Substantial direct assistance is provided for other members of the family of nations, and expenditures in support of our armed forces are materially increased. Funds are included for the necessary strengthening of our economy through the development and conservation of the Nation's productive resources. Increased emphasis is placed on the provision of badly needed measures to promote the education, health, and security of our people.

Showing his basically conservative, middle-course approach to government, Truman used this phrase: "A Government surplus at this time is vitally important to provide a margin for contingencies, to provide reduction of the public debt, to provide an adequate base for the future financing of our present commitments and to reduce inflationary pressures." And he recommended new tax legislation to raise revenues by $4 billion.

It seems to me important in the years ahead to pursue this question of how problems such as the ones just mentioned can be handled by government. While President Truman pursued a middle course, he did work through and strengthen the agencies of the government with economic and budgetary jurisdiction; and he added other institutional arrangements as they were needed. Basically, he felt that as president he had an obligation to furnish management leadership—not to do the whole job of management but to create workable institutional arrangements. That way, cabinet officers and agency heads could get the work done, present their programs to the Congress, handle congressional appropriations, and be responsible to Congress in answering its oversight function. In fact, in the 1950 budget there is a request for $1 million to be appropriated to the president for management improvement.

In the Bureau of the Budget at that time, we had a very active, vigorous, and capable estimates group who dealt with the ongoing programs of each department and agency and who were prepared to offer the president their judgments when needed about the effectiveness of what was being done. There was also a strong legislative liaison section headed by Elmer Staats, who is now comptroller general.

Secretary Snyder has referred to the program of improving the accounting and auditing of the government which he, Lindsay Warren (the comptroller general), and I worked out. Each of us had the power legally to prescribe the accounting and reporting structure of the federal government. Instead of squabbling over the territory, we got together and devised a system that has evolved but is still in existence today as a financial structure of the government.

This basic decision by President Truman to support a rationalization of the government's reporting structure meant that we could compare the financial profile of one year with another and that we could determine what the carryover funds were. This meant that the arguments in Congress over a program—for example, increasing farmlands through irrigation—could focus on facts rather than emotions. In the past those who wanted programs to move forward vigorously would always contend that they were about to run out of money in a very short period of time. Those who wanted to reduce the programs always said, in effect, "There is a lot of money hidden in the desk drawer. The program can continue for the next two or three years without any additional funds." With an accurate set of records, the arguments could center on questions of policy and its implementation.

I would like to mention one other thing in connection with President Truman's understanding of how to use and improve the agencies of government. He was very conscious of the division of powers between the executive and the legislative branches. He knew that he had to supply his leadership within this framework of divided powers.

Specifically I remember that when the Eightieth Congress was elected, Chairman John Taber of the House Appropriations Committee, a very strong and vigorous advocate of reducing government expenditures, proposed that his committee have representatives at the Bureau of the Budget when we made the final budget decisions, so Congress would have adequate information on which to base its work. I am sure Mr. Taber felt that this information would permit him to make substantial reductions. President Truman would have none of this. He said, in effect, "We are the executive branch; we have a responsibility to present the [budgetary] program; we will do so, and Congress has to do its duty in its own way. We will furnish accurate and full information; we will endeavor to give the members of Congress what they need to do their jobs, but we will not mix the executive and legislative functions in this manner." President Truman used the Bureau of the Budget and other mechanisms of the Executive Office to examine the total role of government, its effective performance, and possible improvements.

At the same time, many international matters also required a pulling together, a coordination. It would have been impossible to manage the foreign policy of this country by budgets and dollars; that had to be done by good communications, by understanding the world's leaders. Thus, there was a growing use of the Department of State as a sort of international Bureau of the Budget. All of the interdepartmental committees dealing with international affairs —and at that time there were some forty government agencies dealing with foreign affairs—were chaired by persons in the State Department. The State Department secretariat, which had been established by George Marshall, furnished the secretariat services for each of the interdepartmental coordinating committees; and it was an accepted fact at the time that where the State Department chose to do so, its staff would prepare the first draft of any document or report to come out of a coordinating committee. This gave a cohesion on behalf of the president within the institutional framework. Otherwise matters would have been pursued individually, without a broad national concept of where policies should lead and what would happen once the policy had been agreed to.

As time goes by, historians will give President Truman great credit for these institutional arrangements. Although many of the innovations that were started during his administration have disintegrated or were not modernized, some of today's very successful operations were based on the concepts developed at that time.

ELMER B. STAATS

I shall trace the organization of the Executive Office and of the rest of the president's staff from the standpoint of the integration of economic, social, political, and foreign policies.

After the war, the Office of War Mobilization, which Justice Byrnes had headed, became the Office of War Mobilization and Reconversion. When it was decided to disband that organization, John Steelman was designated assistant to the president; with the aid of Dave Stowe, Harold Enarson, Robert Turner, and many others who were established in the White House staff, Steelman played a key role in the economic conversion program.

The wartime agencies on the economic front were consolidated into the Office of Temporary Controls. This title was, of course, deliberately and specifically selected to emphasize the transitory nature of the residual wartime controls on prices, materials, rents, allocation of resources, and so on. The president selected Gen. Philip Fleming, the former federal works administrator, to head this office. General Fleming did not know anything about controls, but he knew how to take orders, and he knew how to go about organizing an effort of this type. Of course, the Budget Bureau also played an important role, checking to be sure that these control agencies were actually demobilized and that the various residual functions were relocated in the permanent agencies of government.

I think it is worth pointing out that in hindsight the performance of these temporary, wartime agencies was remarkable. We had less than a 2 percent average inflation rate during that period. Considering the pressure on materials and on wages and all of the general dislocations of the wartime economy, the overall record of the 'control agencies on the domestic front was nothing less than miraculous.

For the conversion process a Surplus Property Administration was established, headed by Stuart Symington. It was his first government job, and he played an important part in relieving some of the critical shortages by moving materials and equipment purchased for the war effort back into the private sector. The demobilization of the temporary agencies was largely accomplished by 1948.

This period was also important in integrating the Executive Office staff concerned with economic policy. The Budget Bureau had a Fiscal Policy Division in which Gerhard Colm, Arthur Smithies, and many others played an important part. When the 1946 Employment Act was being considered by Congress, Harold Smith, director of the budget, was rather uncertain about whether to support creation of a separate body that would fashion economic policies and programs. Most of us who had been concerned with the wartime programs advised Smith that we thought it was a good idea. Then after the Council of Economic Advisers came into being, Smithies, Colm, and some others moved from the Bureau of the Budget over to the council.

From the beginning the work of the Budget Bureau was closely integrated with that of the Council of Economic Advisers. This played an important part in establishing what has continued, I think, to be a good relationship between these two elements of the presidential staff. This success was due, in part, to the work of Clark Clifford and of Charlie Murphy: they recognized the need to integrate the staff of the White House itself with the supporting staffs in the Executive Office. There was a considerable movement of personnel—including Dave Bell, Dick Neustadt, Dave Stowe, and many others—from the Budget Bureau to the White House, and this I think also improved communications.

HENRY H. FOWLER

I was deputy administrator of the National Production Authority [NPA] from September 1951 until January 1952 and then administrator from January until June 1952. In June 1952 I was appointed by President Truman to be administrator of the Defense Production Administration and director of the Office of Defense Mobilization; I held these two positions until January 20, 1953.

The economic policies of the Truman administration during this period were largely formulated and developed in the fourteen months following the aggression by North Korea on South Korea (June 1950 to August 1951). The succeeding seventeen months of the Truman administration were marked by some refinement and a dedicated defense and maintenance of those policies, but the basic elements had already been determined. I may claim some objectivity because I was not a member of the administration when these policies were formulated and was concerned only with their management, administration, and maintenance in a later phase.

Now, for a few personal impressions. The economic

policies of this period were not matters of choice by President Truman and his advisers. External circumstances—the aggression by North Korea on South Korea, aided and abetted by the Soviet Union and joined by the People's Republic of China in November 1950—forced their hand. In fact, the defense budget for fiscal year 1951 (beginning July 1, 1950) had shrunk to $13.5 billion, an increase of a mere $100 million over fiscal 1950, despite our entry into NATO in 1949. The mobilization program that was developed in the face of the events of 1950 involved much more than an effort to repel aggression in Korea. It was designed to deter an outbreak of World War III or discourage further aggression on free nations by the heavily armed Communist forces.

The economic policies of the Truman administration during this period were designed to accommodate a rapid build-up of our military forces and those of our allies, to rebuild an adequate mobilization base, and to do so while maintaining the general economy in maximum health.

In his special message to Congress "Reporting on the Situation in Korea" on July 19, 1950, in which he announced his intention to transmit specific requests for additional appropriations, initially totaling $10 billion, President Truman said:

> Our power to join in the common defense rests fundamentally on the productive capacity and energies of our people. In all that we do, therefore, we must make sure that the economic strength which is at the base of our security is not impaired, but continues to grow.

In that same message he outlined with unmistakable clarity exactly what he meant. It is striking in retrospect to see President Truman's early concern that the economy would rapidly become overloaded. He realized that direct measures (priorities and allocations) to assure prompt and adequate supplies for military and essential civilian use would be necessary and that general measures should be devised to compensate for the growth of demand caused by the military programs. Furthermore, Truman saw that the military and mobilization effort would require increased revenues and "pay-as-you-go" financing to reduce the inflationary effects. He emphasized that this tax burden should be fairly distributed; that excessive credit expansion should be restrained; and that various financial, contractual, and related inducements to increase production of essential materials, products, and services should be authorized.

While requesting sensible and restrained action by businessmen, labor, farmers, and consumers, the president announced that "if a sharp rise in prices should make it necessary, I shall not hesitate to recommend the more drastic measures of price control and rationing." In fact, that sharp rise did occur between June and the end of the year, and in January 1951 a full-blown program of wage and price controls was instituted. It substantially flattened out inflation until removed in 1953 by the Eisenhower administration.

There is no more startling example of the value of learning from experience than the performance of the federal government when confronted with the outbreak of hostilities in Korea. There was an immediate recognition of the necessity for another, more limited mobilization to supply both our forces and the UN forces in Korea and, at the same time, to restore America's mobilization after its postwar deterioration. Many individuals in key places in Congress, in the executive branch, and in the private sector had had vivid experiences in organizing production and supply during World War II; and with the erstwhile chairman of the Truman Committee now occupying the White House, an adaptation of proven machinery on a massive scale was put quickly into place.

Within three months of the outbreak of hostilities, Congress had devised and enacted the Defense Production Act of 1950. It contained far more than the authority to direct the economy through priorities, allocations, and wage and price controls. This act provided for government stockpiling of materials through long-term contracts and encouraged additional production capacity by means of related, rapid tax-amortization provisions. The result was a massive expansion of essential materials and facilities. Together with temporary conservation, this gave the United States the ready capability to produce a broad range of critical ma-materials, products, and services that would otherwise have been in short supply. In the event of a broader war than that being waged in South Korea, these measures would have been crucial to the maintenance of an ongoing economy. In the absence of a broader war, this expansion of supply and capacity would make decontrol of the economy feasible in two to three years without damaging the defense effort.

By Executive Order, the president delegated his authority over production and supply to the director of the Office of Defense Mobilization. The director's authority was not limited to exhortation, drawing plans, devising options, or soliciting cooperation for coordinated activities from governmental departments and agencies. He was also given authority "to direct, control, and coordinate" the actions "necessary to assure adequate production and supply." One can only wonder what an adaptation of Truman's policies would have done to solve our energy problems in the 1970s.

The economic policies of the Truman administration were hardly in place before the magnitude of the military challenge took on major proportions. The entry of the Chinese Communists into the fighting in November 1950 increased the danger of a major, all-out war should the Soviet Union be tempted to couple its adventurism in the Far East with action in Berlin or other key points in Western Europe. In the annual budget message for fiscal year 1952, Truman requested $41 billion for the military, compared to $12.3 billion for fiscal year 1950 and $21 billion for fiscal 1951; for international security and foreign relations, the expenditures would increase from $4.8 billion in 1951 to $7.4 billion in 1952. Together, these 1952 requests totaled $48.9 billion or nearly 69 percent of the budget, up 90 percent from fiscal year 1951. One cannot fail to be impressed by the responsible fiscal proposals incorporated in Truman's budget, presented in January 1951, as well as the consistent pay-as-you-go approach emphasized in his special tax message of February 2, 1951.

By the time of the president's message to Congress on April 26, 1951, "Recommending Extension and Broadening of the Defense Production Act," the Truman administration could point to a strong beginning: defense production was under way; the basis had been laid for an effective program to stabilize prices and the cost of living; and the productive capacity for critical materials and products was expanding. Actions on taxes, credit, and price and wage controls had taken hold, arresting the price rise that had marked the period from late June 1950 to January 1951.

The administration offered amendments to strengthen the act, but President Truman, his advisers, and managers found the going rough. Indeed, the opposition in Congress introduced amendments to weaken the act, and a battle royal ensued through the summer until an extension bill, unsatisfactory to the president, became law. From then on, despite further efforts, it was primarily a holding action insofar as the legislative tools of economic policy were concerned.

In conclusion, something should be said about the long hard slog of managing and administering these Truman economic policies. The progress and problems are treated in a series of Quarterly Reports to the president by the Office of Defense Mobilization beginning in the spring of 1951; they cover all aspects of the administration of the Defense Production Act and related legislation. Their titles and dates tell the story:

"Three Keys to Strength," 1951
"Building America's Might," 1951
"Meeting Defense Goals," 1951
"The Battle for Production," 1952
"The Shield against Aggression," 1952
"Strength for the Long Run," 1952
"The Mobilization Readiness Program," 1952
"The Job Ahead," 1953

DAVID H. STOWE

During World War II, we had the War Powers Act, and everything was turned into an aspect of winning the war; but our problem during the Korean War was substantially different. We had to maintain essential defense production while keeping wages and prices stable. In other words, we had to work for guns *and* butter, in view of the fact that we considered ourselves in a limited war.

This created extremely difficult problems, although there had been some planning at the National Security Resources Board. With the outbreak of the fighting in June 1950, there was a great acceleration in U.S. prices, particularly of such things as rubber—and rubber was a very important commodity for us. The increases in prices were paralleled by large increases in wage rates. The result was that during the first six months of the war we had a decidedly inflationary trend. As I recall, the Consumer Price Index rose by about 7.7 percent in an eight-month period. The increase in wage rates, which had been running at about 3.5 percent, went to 6.8 percent in the same period. Finally, in December 1950 the economic stabilization machinery was put in place.

We had a very hot economy: we had a demand market, because people remembered World War II when there was a considerable amount of hoarding; and at the same time wage rates jumped very rapidly for those unions fortunate enough to have contract negotiations during that period. As a matter of fact, some employers were practically begging the unions to take more money in order to ensure enough skilled manpower for stepped-up production.

During the early Korean War period when Alan Valentine was the price stabilizer, there were considerable problems between his office and the Wage Stabilization Board. The latter attempted to work out wage equity for those who had not had raises since the outbreak of the Korean conflict. Regulation 6 ruled that these people could have wage increases of up to 10 percent, a figure the board calculated was the equivalent of the increase in the cost of living plus a fair increment in earnings. Together with the prior wage freeze, this ceiling created the problem; and on about February 15 organized labor withdrew from the Wage Stabilization Board and also withdrew from active participation in many other government agencies. For a period of about a month, labor was on the outside, unwilling to participate because it felt some of the regulations were unfair to its members.

There was a strong feeling at the time that only wages were being controlled, and that other aspects of the economy were not similarly constrained. I think I can say that whatever success we had in the wage stabilization program was not so much due to the brilliance of our staff but rather to what Mike DiSalle did in the price area. Once prices began to come under control and once we got labor back into the government—once labor felt it was getting a fair share and was willing to sacrifice as long as everybody else was too—then the Wage Stabilization Board was able to process nearly sixty thousand cases with few interruptions or disruptions in production. I attribute that to the introduction of price controls: the prices of essential things were held in check. Under those circumstances, labor had no qualms about holding the line on wage rates.

We did have one or two dramatic events during this period. Many people will think of the steel strike, but the question of the price of steel was really of secondary importance. We had already breached the line in some respects with rubber, with copper, with General Electric, so that the actual monetary aspect of the strike was less important than people thought. I suppose the steel strike's greatest claim to fame will be that it tested the power of the president—unfortunately—and from then on, that power was limited by a decision of the Supreme Court.

Nevertheless, the steel strike did create a certain amount of chaos in the Wage Stabilization Board. One of the problems we had was that we had been completely and totally convinced by the Defense Department that even a one-day stoppage of production would create havoc in the Korean War. That prediction subsequently turned out not to be true: the steel strike did not seriously impair the flow of materials to Korea. However, that crisis mentality was typical of those who were advising the president at the time.

The course of events was very quick. The steel workers' contract ran out, and they were free to strike; then President Truman asked them, as a personal favor, not to. Union president Phil Murray, counter to all traditions of the steel workers, then approved some ninety-nine days of production without any contract. When the strike finally did occur, the question arose as to whether the president would invoke the Taft-Hartley Act.

As I recall, the president felt very strongly that since the steel workers had given ninety-nine days of noncontract production, it would be eminently unfair to hit them with another eighty days of mandatory production under Taft-Hartley, especially since it appeared certain that the plants would be shut down after those eighty days.

The wage stabilization program during the Korean War did not have the "no strike, no lockout" commitments that had operated during World War II; all the board had was the cooperation and participation of labor and management and the government. Yet the statistics show unquestionably that the program, with all of its problems, with all of its ups and downs, was eminently successful. Wages were held down; prices were held down; and the type of inflationary spiral that all of us had feared was kept in check. The program worked.

BERTRAM R. GROSS

One of the jokes that was going around Washington in 1946 was: "To err is Truman." But actually the biggest error of the time was committed by the many people—and this surely included some of us working in or close to the

White House—who tried to convert Harry Truman into another F.D.R. or Winston Churchill. It was not until January 1947 and the beginning of the preparations for his reelection campaign that the real Truman spirit came into its own. In that connection I wanted to mention three concepts that seem to fit together.

The first is the Fair Deal. The Fair Deal was different from Wilson's New Freedom or F.D.R.'s New Deal. It was a very far-reaching program and provided 90 percent of everything that appeared later in reprocessed form as the New Frontier and the Great Society. This Fair Deal program, of course, meant that Charlie Brannan was not the only person who was supposed to have received his message from the Kremlin. Indeed, when the full employment bill was first discussed on the Senate floor, Senator Taft said it was taken right from the Soviet constitution.

The second is the Cold War (the first world program for containing communism). It is strange that the leading spokesmen of containment were later attacked as being either traitors or "soft on communism." Another complication was that, even as the containment policy developed on all fronts throughout the world, the loyalty (then called security) program also started. This was one of the most difficult aspects of the Truman administration; and I must say, as I look back on some of the people who were pilloried, I cannot disassociate those attacks from the economic content of the Fair Deal.

Along with the Fair Deal and the containment of communism, the third concept is economic growthmanship. It is not to be found either in Keynes's early treatise on money or in his later work, *The General Theory of Interest, Employment and Money*. In fact, the concept of economic growthmanship, which was indispensible for bringing together the Fair Deal's domestic measures and the creation of a free-world power at the same time, was implicit in much of the debates on the original full employment bill and the 1946 Employment Act. But the theory did not emerge clearly until later.

I recall that in the Council of Economic Advisers we had tremendous difficulties with what I call "the upsy-downsy people." Their approach was that if things went up too far, we would have to bring them down; and if they went down, we would have to bring them up. These people lacked any perspective on the broad process of economic expansion and social growth.

This concept of growth developed in all of the countries of the free world. The Japanese, the British, and the Germans backed into it a different way but in a sense, under American leadership. The other nations had their own functional equivalents of the Executive Office staff with counsel, the Budget Bureau, and the National Security Council. I give no particular credit for leadership to any particular one of these agencies—including the council, where I was working. But economic growth was very much an American concept which then became rather firmly and successfully rooted in Japan and West Germany.

These three policies—a Fair Deal that went beyond immediate political feasibility and provided new foundations for a few decades of subsequent political and economic policies, a coalition of the non-Communist countries to create a free world, and a committed belief in economic growth—these concepts developed during the very rough and controversial period of Truman's administration. If the world, in disarray at the conclusion of World War II, is now organized and stabilized in something of a bipolar sense, with the coalition of Western nations led by the United States, the foundations were laid during the Truman period.

The middle years of the Truman administration are particularly important, because during this period the concepts of the Fair Deal and of broad international expansion were brought together under a philosophy of growth. In a sense, the very nature of Western capitalism changed qualitatively during this period.

Before World War II, before the Truman administration and America's role as a world leader (in part thrust upon us and in part sought), western capitalism had been wracked by catastrophic depressions. Since that time, there has been no catastrophic depression, and I do not think that one is around the corner—even in today's troubled periods. Also, before World War II (at least since 1814), there was never a year without war between at least two of the world's leading capitalist powers or their proxies. One of the things that Marshal Stalin had to unlearn after World War II was the idea that the major capitalist powers would quickly jump into trade wars and then military wars against each other, leaving the Communists to sit back and pick up the pieces. This is no longer the nature of modern capitalism.

I see no possibility, looking very far into the future, of military conflict between any of the leading capitalist powers. And, like the elimination of catastrophic depression, this was one of the major qualitative changes in the nature of western capitalism that emerged during the Truman administration.

12

An Academic Perspective

William J. Barber

Scholars traffic in interpretations, producing a perspective in which to frame events. I am reminded of a young man who joined the staff of a venerable Oxford college to manage its endowment and estates. He discovered, to his surprise, that all of the college's assets were in agricultural land, as they had been since the fourteenth century. When he proposed to the corporate body that stocks and bonds would yield a better rate of return, a senior fellow, horrified, said, "Young man, don't you realize that for six centuries the college has held all its wealth in agricultural land, and it has served us very well?" To which the young man replied, "Yes, sir, but you must realize that the past six centuries have been a very remarkable period." I am told that he made his case.

I suspect that scholars studying economic policy during the Truman presidency will similarly come to regard this phase of our national history as a most remarkable period. Let me suggest a few of the reasons that seem to me to support this conclusion.

In the first place, a sense of the remarkable quality of the Truman administration will no doubt be heightened when our national response to the aftermath of World War II is juxtaposed against our response to World War I. The years 1917 and '18 generated a heady intellectual ferment. Many of the business community's veterans of the War Industries Board and many of the academic sojourners in Washington, who served in government at that time, came away persuaded that the fantastic productive achievements of wartime, under governmental direction, offered lessons for the improved management of the peacetime economy. The writings of Bernard Baruch and some of his associates, as well as those of such economists as Wesley Mitchell, Irving Fisher, and Harold G. Moulton are instructive on this point.

Moulton, incidentally, predicted a new era in the approach to economics as a discipline. Much of the confidence in an imminent fundamental transformation in economics and economic policymaking was blunted, however, by the nation's urge to return to normalcy. But the impetus was not lost entirely; this spirit resurfaced in 1921 when the president's Conference on Unemployment was convened under the leadership of Secretary of Commerce Herbert Hoover. By today's standards the results were modest, but by the standards of the day, it marked an unprecedented departure.

At that conference a novel role for the federal government was asserted, namely as catalyst and coordinator of economic ·activity, especially through the development of countercyclical spending for public works. The lion's share of this spending, however, was to be undertaken by state and local governments. Primarily, the federal role was to provide the economic information that would signal when the tap should be turned off or on.

By contrast, the intellectual ferment generated by World War II—which was nourished also by the experience of the Great Depression—produced quite a different result. In particular, the federal government's formal commitment to maximum levels of income, employment, and purchasing power was embodied in the Employment Act of 1946. Parenthetically, one might predict that the scholar of the next generation is unlikely to be overly exercised by the task of identifying the precise contributions of particular individuals to that transformation. The history of intellectual innovations is filled with instances of simultaneous and independent discoveries. The dominant fact, which will certainly impress itself upon the scholarly community of the future, is that a broad climate for new departures in economic policy had been created. In that respect, the Truman administration was significantly different from anything that had gone before.

But the contrast between our national responses to the rest of the world, and to the termination of hostilities, in 1918 and in 1945 is no less striking. Unlike the 1920s, when we essentially turned our backs on the wider world except to fuss about repayment of war debts, during the Truman years we assumed a responsibility for the world's economic health, and particularly for a devastated Europe. To emphasize the distinctive attribute of that fundamental departure one need only cite Winston Churchill's characterization of the Marshall Plan as "the most unsordid act in history."

It seems reasonable to predict that the student of Truman's economic policies will also find another feature of this period to be remarkable. Not only were the burdens of economic policymaking vastly enlarged, but they were, on the whole, successfully shouldered. As Leon Keyserling has properly emphasized, the overall performance of the economy, as measured by its capacity to create jobs and to increase real output, was strong. There were, to be sure, some bumps along the way—the massive reconversion from war to peace could hardly have been completed smoothly. Nevertheless, neither the widely expected recession nor a deep depression of the 1930s variety occurred.

The added claims on our resources represented by foreign aid programs and by the Korean War mobilization were satisfied without reductions in our standard of living. But the phenomenon which may generate the most puzzlement among the next generation of scholars is why the various policy instruments used in this period took the form they did. Students of economic policymaking are inclined to attempt to seek out formally articulated master models to rationalize the way policies are developed. For some periods, this type of analysis can be fairly readily executed: for example, that kind of procedure explains quite satisfactorily the strategies of economic policy during the Eisenhower and Kennedy administrations.

For the Truman presidency, however, this undertaking appears to be more challenging. It would be tempting to suggest that, at least at the macro-economic level, a Keynesian model would fill this gap. Though a Keynesian ingredient was certainly far from lacking in the thinking of the times, there is undoubtedly more to the story.

Much of the thinking of the first wave of professed Keynesians in this country was organized around the notion of "offsets to saving." That implied that the expected gap between savings and investments would only be closed either by massive programs of public spending or by massive programs of redistributive taxation. But this formulation does not mesh neatly with the strategies that were actually deployed during the Truman years. Nor was there any other standard, textbook teaching available in the 1940s that served ideally as a theoretical guide.

In a number of respects the conceptual innovations to be found, for example, in the internal memoranda and reports of the Council of Economic Advisers were ahead of those in the academic journals. Concepts such as the full employment–balanced budget and the emphasis on economic growth, evident in the work of the Council of Economic Advisers, were in advance of most of the basic theoretical work being done in academia. (Walter Salant has written very effectively* on this aspect of intellectual innovation.) Fertility in economic ideas, of which there was an abundance during this period, is not in itself, however, sufficient to formulate economic policy; the ultimate test is the acceptability of ideas to the president. After all, we do not elect our presidents to be producers of economic ideas; rather, they are consumers of economic ideas. In these matters, most of our presidents have tended to be ardent believers in consumer sovereignty; certainly Franklin Roosevelt was. And

---

* "Some Intellectual Contributions of the Truman Council of Economic Advisers," *History of Political Economy* 5 (1973): 36–49.

furthermore, it was his tendency not to accept any single recommendation whole, but to attempt to blend part of one recommendation with part of another, sometimes in ways that were internally contradictory.

One illustration of this is the discussion that Secretary [of the Treasury Henry] Morgenthau had with Mr. Roosevelt in 1937 about the proposed budget for fiscal year 1938. Mr. Morgenthau presented his estimates of maximum tax revenue, insisted that a balanced budget was imperative, and informed the president that a ceiling on expenditures would have to be established. The president, independently, after meeting with the various spending agencies, found it attractive to trim some but not all requests within the limits Mr. Morgenthau had said were imperative. At a press conference, after his discussion about the expenditure side of the budget, he was asked what the total expected expenditures for the next fiscal year would turn out to be.

The figure appeared in the next day's paper—which Mr. Morgenthau read, not knowing about the president's decision earlier. (This was in the days before the advent of the tape recorder, but Mr. Morgenthau had a stenographer take down all his telephone conversations. The Roosevelt Library yields the following insight.) Secretary Morgenthau phoned the president and announced that he had just learned that the president had obviously ignored his earnest counsel about what would be required to balance the budget. This was outrageous, the secretary continued; he was the president's chief fiscal officer, and he had no alternative but to resign. The rest of the conversation went about as follows: "Now, Henry, you can't do that. You know you are my right hand, but sometimes I keep my left hand under the table."

One gets the impression that President Truman, when dealing with his colleagues and associates, kept both hands on the table, a practice that must surely help account for the intense affection and loyalty he evoked from them.

But like F.D.R., Mr. Truman also appears to have exercised his sovereign powers as a consumer of economic advice—in the views he held on the mix of instruments to conduct economic policy; in his view on the imperative to stabilize the government bond market (a view that implied that monetary policy would be inactive); and in his view that, at least in periods of high income and employment, budget surpluses should be accumulated and used to retire the public debt.

The first of these presidential preferences meant that one of the standard weapons for countering inflation—tight credit—was immobilized. Accordingly, special weight had to be attached to unconventional forms of intervention, such as direct controls. When the authority to deploy these controls was not at hand, success in fighting inflation was compromised. But if the policy mix was not ideal to combat inflation, it may have served the longer-range objective of promoting economic growth. A mix of easy money, tight fiscal policies, and debt retirement is well calculated to encourage capital formation by increasing the availability of funds for private investment on attractive terms.

Moreover, this mix of solutions must have had an attraction for President Truman on other grounds: easy-money policies carry an appealing Populist quality; tight fiscal policies, a ring of conservative orthodoxy. Thus new departures in economic policymaking could be put in place, but continuity with certain well-recognized aspects of our political tradition was also maintained.

Should this line of interpretation be correct, it would suggest that economic policy in the Truman mode was indeed a remarkable blend of economics and politics. Moreover, it would suggest that the student of economic policies during this period might appropriately concentrate at least a substantial part of his energy on discovering the presidential master model of economic growth. It is not to be found in the textbooks, nor, I suspect, is it likely to be found in any single internal memorandum or document. Truman's economic policies, which showed a creative eclecticism, were shaped by a distinctive presidential style; they cannot be explained entirely by the ingenuity of his advisers (notable though that was).

At least two other features of this period will, I suspect,

merit the continuing attention of scholars. One concerns attitudes and strategies that were not immediately translated into programs. Two cases in point are the imaginative approach to agricultural policy, developed by Secretary Brannan, and the long-range view of conservation and public power, advanced by the Department of the Interior (discussed by Mr. Davidson). The fact that these strategies were frustrated does not diminish their interest: they still inspire useful thought on current issues. In short, these initiatives may be regarded by history as productive stillbirths.

A second legacy of these years will certainly capture the attention of future scholars: the major transformation of institutions of economic policymaking and economic management. In the domestic field the most dramatic example was, of course, the creation of the Council of Economic Advisers. But this process extended much more broadly, incorporating the reorganization of other executive departments and agencies (as Mr. Webb and Mr. Staats have reminded us). In international affairs (as noted particularly by Mr. Southard), the task of building institutions made great strides in the development of the Bretton Woods organizations and in the stimulus to shaping the European Economic Community. These institutions have, in fundamental ways, shaped domestic and international economic life for the past quarter of a century or more; and, though modified, they have stood the test of time remarkably well.

13

The Historical Record:
A Bibliographic Essay

Darrel Cady

Harry S. Truman's record as president has been the object of much attention in recent years. Anyone who is at all acquainted with the literature on the Truman presidency is aware of the disagreement among scholars who attempt to appraise the administration's performance in the areas of foreign policy, civil rights, and civil liberties; he also knows of the extensive body of materials that has been produced as a result of this scholarly interest.[1]

Unfortunately, President Truman's domestic economic policies have not attracted as much attention, nor have they generated as much debate. This is not a result of their being inconsequential; instead, it is more reflective of what historians have found interesting or relevant in recent years. Indeed, economic issues were very important during the Truman period, being second only to foreign policy in the administration's concern. They presented the most persistent and often the most vexing domestic problems that Truman faced. Perhaps only when the literature on his economic policies is more complete, and debate has clarified the issues, will it be possible for a much-desired synthesis to be written. In the meantime, it is useful to take stock of the substantial quantity of works that are presently available. Barton Bernstein provided such a service in his comprehensive essay of 1966.[2] Since there is no point in duplicating what he has already done, this essay will call attention only to materials that have been produced since 1966 and will suggest some areas where work is still needed.*

The literature on Truman's economic policies has been affected by the dearth of scholarship on the later Roosevelt years. Domestic developments after 1940 have suffered relative neglect compared to the abundant attention bestowed by historians on Roosevelt's first two terms and on the diplomatic and military aspects of the war years. This is unfortunate for Truman scholars because a greater understanding of the circumstances, the policies, and the programs (or lack thereof) that Truman inherited is a fundamental prerequisite for an adequate assessment of his record, particularly of his first term. A few works produced recently add to our understanding, but many topics and some basic lines of inquiry have yet to be explored.

There is still, for instance, no scholarly history of America's wartime economy, despite its crucial influence on the outcome of the war. John Morton Blum's *V Was for Victory: Politics and American Culture during World War II*† and Richard Polenberg's *War and Society: The United States, 1941–1945* are excellent surveys of wartime America. They provide frameworks for understanding the major economic developments of that era, although their format precludes intensive coverage. Geoffrey Perrett's social history of the period, *Days of Sadness, Years of Triumph: The American People, 1939–1945,* is interesting mainly for its thesis that more change was wrought inadvertently by the war than purposely by the New Deal.

A good starting point for understanding wartime policies would be studies that illuminate the activities of individuals within the Roosevelt administration, but only a handful of such accounts have appeared recently. John Partin's dissertation, " 'Assistant President' for the Home Front: James F. Byrnes and World War II," while sometimes thin on documentation, is nevertheless the most comprehensive

---

* This essay was completed in December 1979 [Ed.].

† A complete bibliography follows the notes to this essay.

of these, largely because Byrnes was involved at the highest policymaking level for most of the war as he oversaw, successively, the administration's stabilization, mobilization, and reconversion efforts. While Partin seems reluctant to render judgments, especially of Roosevelt, the image of Byrnes that emerges is a familiar one—an adjudicator, conservative, generally unsympathetic to labor, deferential to the military and big business, and disinclined to initiate postwar planning. If Byrnes's views on policy reflected Roosevelt's attitudes, Partin does not explicitly say so.

The diaries for the war years of Secretary of the Treasury Henry Morgenthau and Vice-president Henry Wallace are now available. *From the Morgenthau Diaries: Years of War, 1941–1945* is a useful volume mostly for its discussion of problems in financing the war. The entries in *The Price of Vision: The Diary of Henry A. Wallace, 1942–1946* indicate the vice-president's preoccupation with international affairs late in the war and reveal disappointingly little about his thoughts on the postwar domestic economy. The Schapsmeiers's *Prophet in Politics: Henry A. Wallace and the War Years, 1940–1965* suffers the same characteristics as Wallace's diary. Wallace's role as the wartime leader of progressives is described by both Norman Markowitz in *The Rise and Fall of the People's Century: Henry A. Wallace and American Liberalism, 1941–1948* and Alonzo Hamby in *Beyond the New Deal: Harry S. Truman and American Liberalism*. Both make note of the liberals' unrequited loyalty to Roosevelt. Chester Bowles, another leading administration liberal, describes his wartime experiences administering price controls in his memoir, *Promises to Keep: My Years in Public Life, 1941–1969*.

There are even fewer useful studies on members of Congress who tried to influence wartime economic policy. Robert Maddox's dissertation, "Senator Harley M. Kilgore and World War II," covers the liberal senator's efforts, frustrated by conservative colleagues and by the president's private opposition, to secure economic protection for laborers during reconversion. Maddox also describes the efforts of liberal and conservative congressmen to defeat Roosevelt's proposal for national service legislation and Kilgore's attempts to reform the government's wartime research and development policies which favored big business and prestigious private universities. This struggle against established economic and educational power, which went on even after the war, is also discussed in a recent paper by Carroll Pursell, "Alternative American Science Policies during World War II," and by Daniel J. Kevles in his article, "The National Science Foundation and the Debate over Postwar Research Policy, 1942–1945: A Political Interpretation of *Science— The Endless Frontier.*"

Out of the war, too, according to Robert Ficken's dissertation, "The Democratic Party and Domestic Politics during World War II," came a badly deteriorated Democratic party, the result largely of Roosevelt's inattention to its affairs. Ficken also sees the consequent Republican electoral gains during the conflict as foreshadowing their victories in 1946. Robert Garson in *The Democratic Party and the Politics of Sectionalism, 1941–1948,* like Ficken, describes the South beginning to drift away from the Roosevelt coalition even before the war's end, partly because of a perception that labor was gaining greater influence within the party.

In fact, this may have been a misperception. James Foster, who examines the CIO's role in elections between 1944 and 1954 in *The Union Politic: The CIO Political Action Committee,* concludes that the newly created CIO-PAC was ineffective in helping Democrats get elected in 1944. Other recent studies, such as Robert M. McDonald's article, "Collective Bargaining in the Postwar Period," describes the war years as an era of great frustration for labor's rank and file, causing tensions to build under the enforced condition of industrial peace until they were released in the postwar wave of strikes. In "Mobilizing the World War II Economy: Labor and the Industrial Military Alliance," Paul Koistinen criticizes Roosevelt for reversing his prewar, liberal course by subordinating labor to business and the military and for excluding labor from effective influence on war and postwar policies that directly affected its welfare. Nelson N. Lichtenstein concludes in his dissertation, "Industrial Unionism under the No-Strike Pledge: A Study of the CIO during the Second World War," that the CIO leadership's wartime alliance with Roosevelt led to a bureaucratized, devitalized union movement.

Concern for the postwar well-being of labor and other groups led to extensive planning activity and some legislation during the war. The efforts to provide for returning veterans, and the political context in which these efforts occurred, is admirably described by Davis R. B. Ross in *Preparing for Ulysses: Politics and Veterans during World War II.* Philip Warken, in *A History of the National Resources Planning Board, 1933–1943,* confirms the belief that plans issued by the board, which included controversial recommendations for countercyclical spending and a postwar mixed economy, contributed to its abolition in 1943. But this economic planning as well as similar efforts by the Bureau of the Budget had no practical effect; and Patrick Brady in his dissertation, "Toward Security: Postwar Economic and Social Planning in the Executive Office, 1939–1946," contends that it was not because of anti–New Deal attitudes or Roosevelt's disinterest. Brady concludes that for several technical reasons, the procedural and policy outlines were never translated into concrete programs. Conclusions based on a different perspective are offered by Jack S. Ballard in his dissertation, "The Shock of Peace: Military and Economic Demobilization after World War II." After examining preparations for military and economic reconversion, he asserts that the country was well prepared for the readjustment to peacetime circumstances.

One program that clearly was not functioning well when Truman became president was that set up to dispose of surplus property. As Frederick J. Dobney indicates in "The Evolution of Reconversion Policy: World War II and Surplus War Property Disposal," liberals and supporters of small business, veterans, and agriculture combined to alter Roosevelt's conservative-backed plan to dispose of goods on a "business-like" basis. The liberals and their allies wanted to create a multimember board, with social and economic goals in the board's mandate. These changes probably slowed down the actual disposal process, Dobney concludes.

Much of the planning for peace, as in the NRPB report, reflected the beginnings of a sea change in economic thought. That such changes were taking place is well illustrated in Byrd L. Jones's paper, "The Role of Keynesians in Wartime Policy and Postwar Planning, 1940–56," with comments following it by Leon Keyserling, Robert Nathan, and Lauchlin Currie (each of whom helped effect the changes), and in Herbert Stein's *The Fiscal Revolution in America.* The war's vindication of the Keynesian analysis created widespread agreement that the government should play a balancing role in the postwar economy, using fiscal policy to maintain a high level of employment, if not "full" employment. But while a consensus was forming on that goal, agreement on the means to achieve it was not attained. Moreover, most thought was directed toward avoiding a recurrence of prewar economic circumstances rather than coping with the situation Truman was actually to face.

President Truman's economic policies have attracted more scholarly attention recently than those of the war years, but substantially less than other aspects of his administration. What has been produced, however, is usually restricted either topically or in span of time. To date, no general survey devoted solely to a description of economic developments during Truman's presidency has been written, and during the past few years only journalists have produced general accounts of his years in the White House.[3] The most thoroughly researched and best balanced of these, and no doubt the most satisfactory for scholars, is Robert Donovan's *Conflict and Crisis: The Presidency of Harry S. Truman, 1945–1948,* the first of a projected two-volume account of Truman's record. Donovan usefully places economic developments in the context of the president's other concerns and discerningly evaluates Truman's actions.

Many of the problems Truman faced in guiding the

nation through the transition from war to peace are treated in some recent dissertations. George Steinmeyer, in his "Disposition of Surplus War Property: An Administrative History, 1944–1949," describes the difficulties involved in disposing of the vast quantities of surplus war property and in using disposal policies to reduce the power of big business. Jack S. Ballard, in "The Shock of Peace," examines the preparations for military and economic demobilization, against a background of post–World War I and interwar experience, and concludes that the transition was made remarkably well, an accomplishment he believes is not adequately recognized or appreciated by historians. The problems related to disbanding the armed services at the end of the war are described by Bert M. Sharp in " 'Bring the Boys Home': Demobilization of the United States Armed Forces after World War II." In "The Truman Administration's Reconversion Policies, 1945–1947," Darrel Cady suggests that Truman's postwar economic policy, for the short- and long-term, was to avoid a postwar depression and inflation by promoting production and effective demand, with the eventual goal being economic abundance. Truman thereby departed from Roosevelt's restrictionist policies in a manner consistent with contemporaneous liberal thought, Cady indicates, and contributed importantly to postwar prosperity.

The principal threat to prosperity throughout most of Truman's two terms was inflation, an "exceptionally complex" kind of inflation according to Crauford Goodwin and R. Stanley Herren. Their extended essay, "The Truman Administration: Problems and Policies Unfold," is an essential introduction to the administration's efforts to combat this problem. They describe Truman's efforts to employ increased production and wage-price policy as anti-inflation devices, finding fiscal policy to be an undependable tool (due, usually, to a lack of congressional willingness to cooperate in its use). Furthermore, they conclude, "virtually all of the causes of inflation as we understand them today [1974] were discussed within the administration at one time or another" and "almost the whole armory of weapons against inflation was also reviewed and tried."[4] Being one essay in a collection that traces the evolution of postwar wage-price policy into the Nixon administration, Goodwin's and Herren's work has the virtue of placing Truman's record in the context of succeeding administrations', rather than comparing it (as is usually done) to Roosevelt's, which is less analagous. Their essay, however, does not assess the efficacy of Truman's wage-price policies.

The Goodwin-Herren essay also provides the most detailed recent examination of the role played by Truman's Council of Economic Advisers. They credit it with having significant influence on administration policies. Hugh Norton does not: in *The Employment Act and the Council of Economic Advisers, 1946–1976*, a survey of the CEA's activities based on secondary sources, Norton repeats an earlier view that Truman thought of the council as something "nice to have around, . . . but of no real value in a political or operational sense."[5] Truman's second CEA chairman, Leon H. Keyserling, and Walter S. Salant, a CEA economist in the Truman period, claim that the council they were associated with made some important economic innovations. Both Keyserling, in an article entitled "The Council of Economic Advisers since 1946: Its Contributions and Failures," and Salant, in "Some Intellectual Contributions of the Truman Council of Economic Advisers to Policy-Making," mention two concepts the council introduced: setting quantified economic goals and developing the economic growth model. Salant also calls attention to the council's suggestions for greater tax flexibility to compensate for short-run economic fluctuations. While Keyserling criticizes Truman for letting the Federal Reserve Board assume independent authority over monetary policy and for relying excessively upon direct controls to restrain inflation, he praises the results of Truman's economic policies, carried out, he asserts, against inflationary forces as great as any faced by later presidents.

President Truman's performance in attempting to fulfill the general goals of the Employment Act of 1946 are explored in several studies. Wayne D. Lammie examines developments in unemployment and unemployment insurance in his dissertation, "Unemployment in the Truman Administration: Political, Economic, and Social Aspects." Lammie finds that Truman earnestly tried to stimulate employment and to improve unemployment insurance, but Congress posed too many obstacles for him to succeed. John Olson, Jr., in his dissertation, "An Analysis of Fiscal Policy during the Truman Administration (1945–1953)," determines that Truman's use of fiscal policies was imperfect. Postwar production was not stimulated as quickly as was needed, and inflation was not effectively controlled. In "The Truman–80th Congress Struggle over Tax Policy," R. Alton Lee detects in Truman's opposition to a tax-reduction plan by the Republican Congress a happy coincidence of good politics and good economic policy: both the president and the public thought that a tax cut at that time would aggravate inflation. Truman also adopted policies that were both economically sound and politically attractive in responding to the 1948–49 recession, according to William O. Wagnon, Jr., in his dissertation, "The Politics of Economic Growth: The Truman Administration and the 1949 Recession." Selecting a middle way between conservatives, who advocated reductions in taxes and expenditures, and liberals, who counseled increased spending, Truman chose to reverse the downturn by promoting economic growth principally by encouraging business to increase investments. His sensitive response, Wagnon asserts, hastened recovery and successfully met this first test of the Employment Act.

The administration's policies are viewed less favorably by Herbert Stein in his widely noted work *The Fiscal Revolution in America*. His focus is on a change in economic thought that began in the 1930s, leading eventually to the general acceptance of a new economic policy and its great triumph, the tax cut of 1964. A consensus on this new policy emerged during the Truman years, Stein avers, as conservative criticism succeeded in producing "a new version of fiscal and monetary policy . . . from which much of early American Keynesianism had been purged."[6] The administration made no contribution to the development of this consensus; instead, Stein implies, it wrongheadedly pursued a less enlightened course that did not rely so heavily upon fiscal and monetary policies to influence the economy.

Stein also devotes a chapter in his book to the developments which led to the 1951 "accord" that gave the Federal Reserve Board its independence from the Treasury Department in establishing monetary policy. The crucial role of Marriner Eccles, a member of the board and its former chairman, is recounted by Sidney Hyman in *Marriner S. Eccles: Private Entrepreneur and Public Servant;* it contains substantially the same information that Eccles provided earlier in his memoir, *Beckoning Frontiers.* The involvement by Rep. Wright Patman and Sen. Paul Douglas in the dispute between the "Fed" and the Treasury is treated briefly in a 1977 issue of the *Journal of Money, Credit and Banking* in articles by R. E. Weintraub and George S. Tavlas, respectively. Douglas discusses his views on this issue and many others during the Truman era in *In the Fullness of Time: The Memoirs of Paul H. Douglas.*

Truman's labor policies continue to attract more attention than do other economic topics, but notably missing, still, is a thorough study which integrates into a single work a description and evaluation of the administration's policies toward labor throughout both terms. Arthur McClure's monograph, *The Truman Administration and the Problems of Postwar Labor, 1945–1948,* meets this need in part, but no similar work covering the second term is available.

Two labor leaders have been the subjects of recent studies. The most valuable of these is *John L. Lewis: A Biography* by Melvyn Dubofsky and Warren Van Tine. They disclose much about the nature of this most frequent union adversary of Roosevelt's and Truman's and show why Lewis, lacking liberal and labor allies as well as public support, was vulnerable (as other union leaders were not) to the kind of treatment Truman accorded him. Joanna Shurbert's study, "John L. Lewis: The Truman Years," is less useful because she focuses mostly upon Lewis's contributions to the labor movement. Walter Reuther's career is traced in *The Brothers Reuther and the Story of the UAW,* by Victor Reuther, and in *Reuther,* by Frank Cormier and William J. Eaton. The latter work is drawn largely from interviews and an unsystematic selection of non-scholarly secondary sources; Victor's memoir provides a more intimate account of his brother's views and activities, but references to Truman's policies are rare.

    Truman and Taft-Hartley: A Question of Mandate, by R. Alton Lee, is the most comprehensive treatment of the circumstances leading to passage of the "slave-labor law" and of the subsequent efforts to alter or repeal it. Lee portrays Truman as being generally loyal to an urban-industrial, labor constituency, on which he depended for reelection, but unable to overcome the influence on labor legislation of the anti-labor, middle class–agrarian–business constituency of Congress. Additional dimensions of the conflict between organized labor and conservative forces in society through 1948 are provided in dissertations by Ronald Templeton, "The Campaign of the American Federation of Labor and the Congress of Industrial Organizations to Prevent Passage of the Labor-Management Relations Act of 1947," and George Roukis, "American Labor and the Conservative Republicans, 1946–1948: A Study in Economic and Political Conflict." Templeton describes what he concludes was a futile campaign by labor to prevent passage of the Taft-Hartley Act. Roukis examines the efforts of labor to combat the broader, conservative economic program of Eightieth-Congress Republicans and calls attention to labor's alternative, which emphasized the maintenance of consumers' purchasing power. Developments in Congress involving passage of the Taft-Hartley Act are also covered briefly in two excellent works devoted to larger subjects, Susan Hartmann's *Truman and the 80th Congress* and James T. Patterson's *Mr. Republican: A Biography of Robert A. Taft.*

    The only other aspect of the administration's labor policies to attract substantial scholarly attention in recent years is Truman's intervention in labor-management disputes, particularly in the steel industry. Several instances of such involvement are analyzed by Arthur Schaefer in his dissertation, "Presidential Intervention in Labor Disputes during the Truman Administration: A History and Analysis of Experience." He seeks to determine what factors motivated intervention, what powers Truman had available to him when he became involved, and what techniques he used in intervening. In "Collective Bargaining in Basic Steel and the Federal Government, 1945–1960," Richard Nagle examines the government's role in four postwar steel disputes, three of which occurred during the Truman period (1946, 1949, 1952), to determine the reasons for and consequences of federal involvement. The administration's intervention in the steel dispute of 1952 is examined most closely in Maeva Marcus's splendid study, *Truman and the Steel Seizure Case: The Limits of Presidential Power*. Her emphasis, however, is on the separation-of-powers issue that the seizure raised and the Supreme Court's decision which served as a check on the accretion of power by modern presidents, rather than the economic problems or policies involved (although substantial information on the latter is included). Readers of the Marcus study should also examine *Presidential Seizure in Labor Disputes* by John L. Blackman, Jr. This work provides an excellent historical analysis of the seventy-one occasions on which presidents, beginning with Abraham Lincoln, seized industrial property. It thereby provides a perspective that makes Truman's action to resolve the steel crisis and other emergency disputes seem less a misuse of power than it is sometimes considered. Secretary of Commerce Charles Sawyer, who was in charge of the seized mills in 1952, describes the developments from his viewpoint in his autobiography, *Concerns of a Conservative Democrat*.[7] In an article by Phillip Stebbins, "Truman and the Seizure of Steel: A Failure in Communications," the administration's defeat in the Supreme Court is seen as the result of Truman's inability to convince the public and the Court that a real crisis, necessitating such action, existed. In " 'Draft the Strikers (1946) and Seize the Mills (1952)': The Business

Reaction," Thomas DiBacco concludes that since it supported the 1946 threat but opposed the 1952 seizure, business was less concerned about the constitutionality of the means Truman employed than about who would be affected.

The administration's migratory labor policies receive some attention in Richard B. Craig's *The Bracero Program: Interest Groups and Foreign Policy*. While the book is constructed as a case study of interest-group conflict and diplomacy relating to Mexican migrant-labor programs between 1942 and 1965, it provides a substantial amount of historical information as well as a useful bibliography. More limited in scope is Peter Kirstein's recent article, "Agribusiness, Labor, and the Wetbacks: Truman's Commission on Migratory Labor." Kirstein examines the "noble but futile effort" of the administration and the commission to resolve differences over Mexican labor between agri-business and organized labor.

Although few historians have devoted attention to the administration's agricultural policies, coverage of its record in that area is relatively good. There are two commendable surveys which describe developments through 1948 especially well, though from different interpretive perspectives. In *Farm Policies and Politics in the Truman Years*, Allen Matusow examines the principal agricultural issues in a political context, slighting somewhat the post–1948 developments. The administration's first-term policies are explored more thoroughly by James Forsythe in his dissertation, "Clinton P. Anderson: Politician and Businessman as Truman's Secretary of Agriculture." Forsythe's work suggests that readers should reconsider assertions by Matusow and Barton Bernstein that Secretary Anderson was largely responsible for the termination of price controls in 1946 and should also question Bernstein's uncritical praise of Stabilization Director Chester Bowles.[8] Anderson briefly describes his own experience as secretary and his senatorial opposition to the program by his successor, Charles Brannan, in his memoir, *Outsider in the Senate: Senator Clinton Anderson's Memoirs.*

Some indications of Southern influence on farm policy during the Truman era can be gleaned from two articles in a recent issue of *Agricultural History,* one by Theodore Saloutos, "Agricultural Organizations and Farm Policy in the South after World War II," and another by Edward L. and Frederick H. Schapsmeier, "Farm Policy from FDR to Eisenhower." Useful too for the data they contain are *American Farm Policy, 1948–1973,* by Willard W. Cochrane and Mary E. Ryan, and especially Volume 4 of *Agriculture in the United States: A Documentary History,* edited by Wayne D. Rasmussen.

The impact of economic policies and circumstances on the political process during the Truman years is demonstrated in several recent works. James R. Boylan concludes in his dissertation, "Reconversion in Politics: The New Deal Coalition and the Election of the Eightieth Congress," that the Republicans' congressional victories in 1946 were the result of voter reaction to short-term reconversion issues, not voter rejection of the long-term social-welfare goals of the New Deal. That was not the case in the South, however, according to Robert A. Garson who traces the gradual alienation of southern Democrats from the national party in *The Democratic Party and the Politics of Sectionalism, 1941–1948,* indicating that the estrangement was due not only to differences on racial questions but on fundamental economic issues as well. In Susan Hartmann's fine study, *Truman and the 80th Congress,* it is also evident that the president differed most sharply with that Congress over domestic economic issues and that Truman's inability to get liberal legislation enacted was due in part to the postwar prosperity which diminished the New Deal constituency's support for change.

The influence of economic issues on the outcome of the 1948 election is treated in many works. Matusow and Forsythe, for example, discuss the effect of agricultural issues; McClure and Lee appraise the influence of labor policies; Garson relates the concerns of the South; Hartmann describes Truman's use of the record of the Eightieth Congress; Alonzo

Hamby examines the issues in the context of his study of liberalism; and Clayton Koppes, in "Conservation and the Continuity of American Liberalism, 1933–1953," and Elmo Richardson, in *Dams, Parks, & Politics,* discuss the influence of resource policy on the outcome of the election.

The best overall analysis of the contest is provided by Richard Kirkendall in "Election of 1948." It was a "maintaining" election, he observes, in which Truman's use of domestic economic issues was important in securing the victory by reassembling the New Deal coalition—including urban workers and voters in the Midwest, far West, and the South. The role of the CIO Political Action Committee in this election, as well as others from 1944 to 1954, is assessed by James C. Porter in *The Union Politic.* Irwin Ross provides a narrative of developments in *The Loneliest Campaign: The Truman Victory of 1948* and attempts to determine how influential the farm vote was by analyzing returns in twelve Midwest and western states. Robert Shogan's article, "1948 Election," constitutes a good brief account. Two relevant dissertations are Ann C. Hasting's "Intraparty Struggle: Harry S. Truman, 1945–1948" and Harold Wallace's "The Campaign of 1948." Allan Yarnell's *Democrats and Progressives: The 1948 Election as a Test of Postwar Liberalism* focuses on the impact of Henry Wallace's candidacy, asserting that it did not force Truman to shift to the left. Wallace's attempt to rally liberals behind a third-party banner and his role in the election are treated in the Schapsmeiers' book, *Prophet in Politics,* and in Norman Markowitz's *The Rise and Fall of the People's Century.* The record and views of Wallace's running mate, Sen. Glen Taylor, are similarly described in F. Ross Peterson's *Prophet without Honor: Glen H. Taylor and the Fight for American Liberalism.*

While the Wallace-Taylor challenge was motivated largely by differences with the administration over foreign policy, there was then—and there remains now—a question of how faithfully Truman fulfilled his New Deal legacy. Some important works have appeared recently which explore the administration's place in the liberal tradition. One which finds continuity between the New Deal and the Fair Deal is Alonzo Hamby's *Beyond the New Deal*. Hamby extensively analyzes the relationship between Truman and active liberals from the war years to 1953. The administration's major economic concerns—such as the Employment Act, the Brannan Plan, growth economics, and developments during the Korean War—are discussed, leading Hamby to conclude that Truman "advanced and even added to the New Deal heritage with his management of the economy."[9] In *Toward a Planned Society: From Roosevelt to Nixon,* Otis Graham attempts to trace the use of economic planning in successive administrations. He contends that unlike Roosevelt, Truman was not receptive to planning concepts, and consequently, Truman and Fair Deal liberals advanced only the broker-state arrangements of the 1930s.

Clayton Koppes questions the notion of continuity between the New Deal and the Fair Deal more directly as he examines the administration's policies toward dependent people and resource policy in his dissertation, "Oscar Chapman: A Liberal at the Interior Department, 1933–1953." In "Public Water, Private Land" and "Conservation and the Continuity of American Liberalism," Koppes suggests that Chapman—a leading New Dealer, 1944 Wallace supporter, and Truman's secretary of the interior from 1949 to 1953—symbolizes continuity. Yet together, Koppes argues, Chapman and the administration developed resource policies that departed from the New Deal goals of redistributing economic and social power and maintaining a balance between development and preservation. The Fair Dealers sought, instead, goals of abundance and national security that were to be reached through economic growth, with a preference for development over preservation. This not only represents discontinuity, Koppes asserts, but also a transformation of American liberalism: the social vision and spiritual concerns of New Dealers were replaced by mid-century with a "hardened" liberalism, a change epitomized by Chapman and the administration's resource policy.

Koppes's works are part of only a few, recent efforts to explore resource policy. More attempts will appear, undoubtedly, as scholars examine past policies that are related to the resource and environmental problems that emerged in the 1960s and 1970s. These scholars will profit if they begin by consulting the excellent assessment of primary sources provided by Elmo Richardson near the end of *Dams, Parks & Politics: Resource Development & Preservation in the Truman-Eisenhower Era*. This work, based on extensive use of those sources, describes the policies and politics of efforts by the Truman administration to establish a Columbia Valley Authority, the controversy over the proposal to build the Echo Park Dam, and the conflicts that arose over attempts to open federal lands for greater exploitation. In *The Bureau of Reclamation,* William E. Warne, former assistant commissioner of reclamation and assistant secretary of the interior during the Truman period, provides a general introduction to the functions, problems, and accomplishments of the Interior Department's best-funded agency. The bureau's actions to maintain the 160-acre law, administrative in-fighting over the valley authority issue, and the bureau's struggles against preservationists are presented in greater detail by David Kathka in his dissertation, "The Bureau of Reclamation in the Truman Administration: Personnel, Politics, and Policy." Development of the Missouri Basin Inter-Agency Committee to coordinate the Pick-Sloan plan is traced by John R. Ferrell in "Water in the Missouri: The Inter-Agency Concept at Mid-Century."[10]

One aspect of the administration's resource policy that is certain to be examined more closely in the future is treated briefly by Gerald D. Nash in his *United States Oil Policy, 1890–1964*. In surveying federal oil and natural gas policies, Nash suggests that Truman, frustrated on the tidelands issue and the oil-depletion allowance, and in his effort to revive antitrust policy, ended up helping to consolidate an understanding arranged with business in the New Deal whereby the government served as arbiter in a system of regulated competition. This arrangement, Nash concludes, typified the new cooperative relationship that was developing between government and big business. Two additional studies that include some useful information are Arthur M. Johnson's *Petroleum Pipelines and Public Policy, 1906–1959* and E. Anthony Copp's *Regulating Competition in Oil: Government Intervention in the U.S. Refining Industry, 1948–1975*.

Aside from these works, historians have produced little that examines in detail the administration's policies toward specific industries or, for that matter, business in general. One interesting and rather unique work that reveals business-men's opinions of and reactions to government policies and economic problems is Herman Krooss's *Executive Opinion: What Business Leaders Said and Thought, 1920s–1960s*. A work that describes the evolution of views of an organization made up mostly of businessmen is Karl Schriftgiesser's *Business and Public Policy: The Role of the Committee for Economic Development, 1942–1967*. Two studies are also available that deal with Truman's relations with the commissions that regulated business. Donald Whitnah's *Safer Skyways: Federal Control of Aviation, 1926–1966* provides some information on Truman's involvement in aviation matters, particularly with the Civil Aeronautics Board, and on efforts to better regulate the growing industry. More helpful in terms of Truman's policies is Gale E. Peterson's dissertation, "President Harry S. Truman and the Independent Regulatory Commissions, 1945–1952." Peterson maintains that Truman sincerely pursued a New Deal–Fair Deal philosophy, vigorously used his appointment and budgeting powers, and in nearly every commission sought greater administrative efficiency and broader powers.

Statistical information about the backgrounds, time in office, and later careers of top political executives in the Truman administration is analyzed and compared to similar data on appointees of other presidents from Roosevelt to Johnson in David T. Stanley, Dean Mann, and Jameson Doig, *Men Who Govern: A Biographical Profile of Federal Political Executives*. This kind of information has been supplemented now in a new publication which historians will welcome, *Political Profiles: The Truman Years,* edited by Eleanora Schoenebaum. It contains political biographies of 435 persons who significantly influenced national affairs between 1945 and 1952. Other biographical works and memoirs of members of the administration or of Congress include: William O. Wagnon, Jr., "John Roy Steelman: Native Son to Presidential Adviser"; Theodore Rosenof, "The Economic Ideas of Henry Wallace, 1933–1948"; Samuel B. Hand, *Counsel and Advice: A Political Biography of Samuel I. Rosenman;* Alexander R. Stoesen, "The Senatorial Career of Claude D. Pepper"; Kenneth D. Hairgrove, "Sam Rayburn: Congressional Leader, 1940–1952"; J. Joseph Huthmacher, *Senator Robert P. Wagner and the Rise of Urban Liberalism;* and Alfred Steinberg, *Sam Rayburn: A Biography.*

It is plain from the foregoing survey that a great deal has already been written that bears upon the economic policies of Roosevelt and Truman. More is needed, however, before a valid assessment of Truman's record can be made. It would be useful to know more about the policies and circumstances Truman inherited from Roosevelt and whether F.D.R.'s policies helped or hindered Truman. For example, one line of inquiry might proceed this way: Were Truman's troubles during his first eighteen months in office largely the result of Roosevelt's failure to prepare adequately for the transition to peacetime conditions? Or, more specifically, could the postwar wave of strikes, and conceivably even the Taft-Hartley Act, have been avoided if Roosevelt's wartime labor policies were more equitable? Could postwar inflation have been more manageable if Roosevelt had not lost control of his party in Congress (and hence of wartime tax policy) or if the public and interest groups had been prepared in advance, while wartime unity still made it possible, to accept postwar economic restraints until conditions stabilized?

As another example, Truman's record is often evaluated in terms of how well he defended, consolidated, or extended Roosevelt's New Deal. Before such an assessment is made, it would seem to be necessary to know to what extent Roosevelt's wartime policies weakened his own coalition, enfeebled the Democratic party, diminished liberal influence, and restored the "economic royalists" to positions of power and prestige. It might also be instructive to compare Roosevelt's record in protecting his own New Deal from being unraveled by the Seventy-seventh and Seventy-eighth Congresses with similar efforts made later by Truman. While these questions are only suggestive, more like them need to be asked and pursued. There should be a clear understanding of what Truman inherited before his record is appraised.

There is, thus, an obvious need for an examination of Roosevelt's wartime economic policies, a thorough study of politics as they relate to economic issues during the conflict, and a general history of the wartime economy. A study of wartime relations between Congress and the executive branch would also be helpful, as would an examination of the role and activities of some of the more influential individuals within the administration and Congress.

The fifty-three civilian control agencies and their activties have also suffered scholarly neglect, except for a few early and now inadequate official histories. Especially useful would be studies of the War Manpower Commission, the Office of Price Administration, the War Production Board, and a new history of the Office of War Mobilization and Reconversion.[11] The wartime roles of most of the executive branch departments, their subdivisions, and independent agencies need to be revealed too. Some insights might be obtained into how industrial and other private interests quietly regained their influence in formulating public policy during and after the war by studying the privately financed, quasi-governmental, sometimes secretive National Petroleum Council, Business Advisory Council, and similar groups that worked closely with federal departments and agencies.[12]

A few of the many other topics that need exploration include: Roosevelt's efforts to obtain national service legislation; the record (or lack thereof) of the Retraining and Reemployment Administration; food policy; the dispute over research and development policy; the war's impact on large and small businesses; resource policy; the wartime activities of special interest groups; and the evolution of economic thought during the war.

It would be instructive, too, if an effort were made to determine what Truman's economic knowledge and philosophy was when he entered the White House, perhaps as Daniel R. Fusfeld did for Roosevelt.[13] Crauford D. Goodwin and R. Stanley Herren describe Truman as "untrained even in the rudiments of economics."[14] If they mean formal training, they are, of course, correct. But what of his practical knowledge? His adult experiences were varied: he had worked for a railroad and a bank; farmed for a decade; done military service; had investments; owned a retail business; been a political administrator in a rural-metropolitan county; been a salesman; as a senator, been interested in railroads; and, of course, was familiar with the wartime economy because of his chairmanship of the Truman Committee. It is possible that he had a better understanding of how the American economy actually works than most twentieth-century presidents.

Also, what was Truman's economic philosophy? Was he a liberal, a conservative, a Populist, or some combination of each? How were his values influenced by his years as a corn-belt farmer, his experiences as an owner of a small business, his growing up during the years of the Populist movement adjacent to a center of its strength, or his border-state heritage? A good scholarly biography will answer most of these questions. At any rate, a better understanding of his economic knowledge and philosophy will provide for a more accurate assessment of his presidency.

Clearly, the most useful project that needs to be done on Truman's presidency is a comprehensive examination of his economic policies throughout both terms. It may be some time before such a synthesis appears, however, because of the gaps in the literature upon which such a work must depend. Meanwhile, there are a large number of worthwhile studies to be undertaken that would contribute to that end.

One such project might be to make an objective examination of the quality of Truman's appointees, particularly of those persons upon whom he depended for economic advice. Was there a "reincarnation of the Harding courthouse gang," as Harvard Sitkoff has suggested?[15] Did Truman appoint and depend upon "cronies," as is so often charged, any more than any other president, including Roosevelt? Were Fred Vinson and John Snyder, for example, less competent than Henry Morgenthau as secretary of the treasury; were W. Averell Harriman and Charles Sawyer more conservative than Jesse Jones in the Commerce Department; were Clinton P. Anderson and Charles Brannan less capable than Claude Wickard in the Department of Agriculture? A comparison of Truman's major appointees to those of Presidents Roosevelt or Eisenhower might be revealing.

Another assumption that is widely expressed but which has never been subjected to close scrutiny is the assertion that shortly after the war "New Dealers left the government in droves" because they despaired of Truman's lack of commitment to liberal reform.[16] Was there such an exodus, or was it just part of the movement of some half a million civilians who left government employment in late 1945? If liberals did abandon the administration, what were their motives? Was it disaffection with Truman's policies? Were they just tired after long years of federal service? Or were they leaving for jobs in universities or business that had not been available for fifteen years?

Other useful studies, in no particular order, might include an examination of the readjustment experiences of war workers and of veterans to help explain why that process occurred so smoothly.[17] A brief account of the United States Employment Service's contribution to high postwar employment might be useful too. An investigation of the politics surrounding the demise of the Office of Price Administration is needed. The railroad strike of 1946 needs to be examined more closely than it has been to determine why Truman acted so tough. The economic and political aspects of the 1952 steel strike bear scrutiny, too, as do some other strikes.

(Scholars must be careful, however, not to assume that actions relating to specific strikes reveal fully the administration's policies toward labor or business). Of course, we lack a study of the administration's labor policies during the second term. A review of the administration's policies toward migratory labor would also be helpful, as would a description and evaluation of the depressed areas program.

A single study explaining all of the wide variety of techniques used by the administration to combat inflation is needed. Fiscal and wage-price policies have received attention while credit controls and other aspects of monetary policy have been neglected. Such a work should be interesting in view of Truman's determination not to use interest rates to counteract inflation. The effectiveness of the techniques that were used merits analysis. Comparing them to the less successful governmental efforts to combat inflation during the 1970s might be enlightening, too. The political circumstances surrounding the 1951 "accord" which restored the Federal Reserve Board's authority over monetary policy needs investigation. An explanation of the role of the banking industry and the part played by some congressmen in this development should be part of such a study. In view of its long-term consequences, the "accord" is possibly the most underrated event of the Truman period.

The administration's second-term agricultural policies need additional attention. Studies of the influence on policy and programs by the National Farmers Union, the Grange, and especially the Farm Bureau Federation would be valuable. The accomplishments and implications of the Rural Electrification Administration's role in extending electrical and telephone services in the countryside need to be explored too.

In view of the current increasing interest in the availability of natural resources, it might be instructive to reexamine the oil-depletion allowance and the offshore oil controversies of the Truman period, using archival sources that were not available when earlier studies were made.

Natural gas policy needs to be reviewed, as well as federal policies toward the oil, lumber, and mining industries.

There are virtually no studies of the administration's policies toward business in general or toward specific industries; that relationship as much as any other needs greater attention. The effect upon the domestic economy of foreign aid programs, particularly the Marshall Plan, and of foreign policy in general needs to be illuminated. The influence on economic policy and legislation wielded by the National Association of Manufacturers and the United States Chamber of Commerce has not been explored. Of special interest would be a description of their roles in the death of the Office of Price Administration and in the passage of the Taft-Hartley Act. Very little has been written to explain what happened in the military-industrial complex during the period of low military budgets between the end of World War II and the start of the Korean War.[18]

More needs to be known about postwar government research and development policies and about the influence on the postwar economy of the technology that had been developed during the war. A study of the struggle to create the National Science Foundation and of its early policies would also be a worthwhile contribution.[19]

The role of economic issues in the 1946 and 1948 elections warrants further clarification: apparently, they were crucial in both contests. Historians are inclined to blame Truman for the 1946 loss, but they seem reluctant to give him full credit for the 1948 upset, perceiving it instead as a mandate for continuing Roosevelt's policies and maintaining New Deal programs even though the New Deal had been moribund for a decade. An analysis of Truman's victory may indicate that he, more than Roosevelt, represented a brand of politics that voters in the Midwest and West could respond to, at least in 1948.

Almost all aspects of the administration's policies during the Korean War need to be investigated more thoroughly. The records of the Korean War stabilization agencies, like their World War II counterparts, have not been extensively used. An explanation of the administration's success in controlling inflation during the conflict would be an important contribution.[20]

Biographical studies such as Clayton Koppes's work on Oscar Chapman and James Forsythe's on Clinton P. Anderson have proven to be interesting and worthwhile additions to our knowledge of resource and agricultural policies, respectively. Similar studies of Charles Brannan, John Snyder, Chester Bowles, John Steelman, Clark Clifford, and many others in the administration who influenced the formulation of economic policy could improve our understanding of Truman's policies.

When some of these topics are treated, along with others, it may be possible to make a judicious appraisal of Truman's record in dealing with economic problems. No appraisal will really be valid, however, if scholars continue to ignore Leon Keyserling's frequent stricture to include in their evaluation of economic policies an assessment of the policies' results. Only by assessing performance is the worth of such policies measured.[21]

NOTES

1. Richard S. Kirkendall, ed., *The Truman Period as a Research Field* (Columbia: University of Missouri Press, 1967); Richard S. Kirkendall, ed., *The Truman Period as a Research Field: A Reappraisal, 1972* (Columbia: University of Missouri Press, 1974). For some recent review articles see: Robert Griffith, "Truman and the Historians: The Reconstruction of Postwar American History," *Wisconsin Magazine of History* 59 (Autumn 1975): 20–50; Richard Polenberg, "Historians and the Liberal Presidency: Recent Appraisals of Roosevelt and Truman," *South Atlantic Quarterly* 75 (Winter 1976): 20–35; Geoffrey S. Smith, " 'Harry, We Hardly Know You': Revisionism, Politics and Diplomacy, 1945–1954," *American Political Science Review* 70 (June 1976): 560–82; Athan Theoharis, "The Truman Presidency: Trial

and Error," *Wisconsin Magazine of History* 55 (Autumn 1971): 49–58.

2. Barton J. Bernstein, "Economic Policies," in *The Truman Period as a Research Field,* ed. Kirkendall, pp. 87–148.

3. A description and econometric analysis of early postwar economic activity is provided in Conrad A. Blyth, *American Business Cycles, 1945–1950* (New York: Praeger, 1969); Harold G. Vatter provides a readable survey in *The U.S. Economy in the 1950s: An Economic History* (New York: Norton, 1963); Cabell Phillips, *The Truman Presidency: The History of a Triumphant Succession* (New York: Macmillan, 1966), describes economic developments into 1946 and in connection with the 1948 election but disregards them thereafter; Bert Cochran provides a critical account that also devotes little space to economic policy, especially after 1948, in *Harry S. Truman and the Crisis Presidency* (New York: Funk & Wagnalls, 1973); the spirit of the times is conveyed in Joseph C. Goulden, *The Best Years, 1945–50* (New York: Atheneum, 1976); Donald R. McCoy at the University of Kansas is preparing a study of the Truman period for the American Presidency Series of the Regents Press of Kansas.

4. Crauford D. Goodwin and R. Stanley Herren, "The Truman Administration: Problems and Policies Unfold," in *Exhortation and Controls: The Search For a Wage-Price Policy, 1945–1971,* ed. Crauford Goodwin (Washington, D.C.: The Brookings Institution, 1975), pp. 90–93; see also Carl A. Auerbach, "Presidential Administration of Prices and Wages," *George Washington Law Review* 35 (December 1966): 191–201, and Daniel Quinn Mills, *Government, Labor, and Inflation: Wage Stabilization in the United States* (Chicago: University of Chicago Press, 1975), pp. 23–36.

5. Hugh S. Norton, *The Employment Act and the Council of Economic Advisers, 1946–1976* (Columbia: University of South Carolina Press, 1977), p. 125.

6. Herbert Stein, *The Fiscal Revolution in America* (Chicago: University of Chicago Press, 1969), p. 461.

7. Sawyer disputes as "pure fiction" Richard Neustadt's assertion that Sawyer failed to cooperate with Truman in an attempt to settle the strike. Maeva Marcus finds that the evidence tends to support Sawyer, not Neustadt. See Charles Sawyer, *Concerns of a Conservative Democrat* (Carbondale: Southern

Illinois University Press, 1968), pp. 274–77; Richard E. Neustadt, *Presidential Power: The Politics of Leadership* (New York: Wiley, 1969), pp. 22–25; Maeva Marcus, *Truman and the Steel Seizure Case: The Limits of Presidential Power* (New York: Columbia University Press, 1977), pp. 289–90n.

8. Barton J. Bernstein, "Clash of Interests: The Postwar Battle between the Office of Price Administration and the Department of Agriculture," *Agricultural History* 41 (January 1967): 45–57; Barton J. Bernstein, "The Postwar Famine and Price Control, 1946," *Agricultural History* 38 (October 1964): 235–40. Bowles blames himself for losing vital southern support in Congress when he imposed price ceilings on raw cotton early in 1946: Chester Bowles, *Promises to Keep: My Years in Public Life, 1941–1969* (New York: Harper & Row, 1971), pp. 174–84.

9. Alonzo Hamby, *Beyond the New Deal: Harry S. Truman and American Liberalism* (New York: Columbia University Press, 1973), p. 514.

10. Some guides to the literature include: Denton E. Morrison, Kenneth E. Hornback, and W. Keith Warner, comps., *Environment: A Bibliography of Social Science and Related Literature* (Washington, D.C.: G.P.O., 1973); Denton E. Morrison, comp., *Energy: A Bibliography of Social Science and Related Literature* (New York: Garland, 1975); Lawrence B. Lee, "100 Years of Reclamation Historiography," *Pacific Historical Review* 47 (November 1978): 507–64; Gordon B. Dodds, "Conservation and Reclamation in the Trans-Mississippi West: A Critical Bibliography," *Arizona and the West* 13 (Summer 1971): 143–71.

11. For additional suggestions regarding topics and sources see: Albert A. Blum, "Mobilization of Men and Machines during the Second World War," in *World War II: An Account of its Documents*, ed. James E. O'Neill and Robert W. Krauskopf. (Washington, D.C.: Howard University Press, 1976), pp. 183–88; and Joseph Howerton, "The Record of Federal Emergency Civilian Control," *ibid.*, pp. 189–210.

12. For additional suggestions see: Jim F. Heath, "Domestic America during World War II: Research Opportunities for Historians," *Journal of American History* 58 (September 1971): 384–414.

13. Daniel R. Fusfeld, *The Economic Thought of Franklin D.*

Roosevelt and the Origins of the New Deal (New York: Columbia University Press, 1956).

14. Goodwin and Herren, "The Truman Administration," p. 37.
15. Harvard Sitkoff, "Years of the Locust: Interpretations of the Truman Presidency since 1965," in *The Truman Period as a Research Field: A Reappraisal, 1972,* ed. Kirkendall, p. 89.
16. Barton J. Bernstein, "America in War and Peace," in *Towards a New Past: Dissenting Essays in American History,* ed. Barton J. Bernstein (New York: Pantheon, 1968), p. 301. Richard Polenberg indicates that much of the exodus occurred during the war: *War and Society: The United States, 1941–1945* (Philadelphia: Lippincott, 1972), pp. 90–91.
17. A plea for more working class history is made by James Green in "Working Class History in the 1940s: A Bibliographical Essay," *Radical America* 9 (July-August 1975): 206–13.
18. Truman was instrumental in creating the postwar link between the military and the aviation industry, according to Donald J. Mrozek, "The Truman Administration and the Enlistment of the Aviation Industry in Postwar Defense," *Business History Review* 48 (Spring 1974): 73–94. Murray L. Weidenbaum indicates that corporate profits after taxes went down during both World War II and the Korean War: "The Need for Reframing the M-I Relationship," in *The Political Economy of the Military-Industrial Complex,* ed. Warren F. Ilchman and Joe S. Bain (Berkeley: University of California Press, 1973), pp. 55–94. James Martin Cypher, "Military Expenditures and the Performance of the Postwar U.S. Economy," (Ph.D. dissertation, University of California, Riverside, 1973) was not available for this essay. Some literature is listed in Thomas A. Meeker, comp., *The Military-Industrial Complex: A Source Guide to the Issues of Defense Spending and Policy Control* (Los Angeles: California State University, 1973).
19. Milton Lomask, *A Minor Miracle: An Informal History of the National Science Foundation* (Washington, D.C.: G.P.O., 1976) contains some information.
20. John E. Wiltz, "The Korean War and American Society," in *The Korean War: A 25-Year Perspective,* ed. Francis H. Heller (Lawrence: Regents Press of Kansas, 1977), pp. 112–58, provides a general overview.
21. Leon Keyserling, "Comments," *ibid.,* pp. 174–79.

Bibliography

Editor's Note: This bibliography was prepared by Darrel Cady.

Adams, Leonard P. *The Public Employment Service in Transition, 1933–1968: Evolution of a Placement Service into a Manpower Agency.* Ithaca: New York State School of Industrial and Labor Relations, 1969.

Anderson, Clinton P. *Outsider in the Senate: Senator Clinton P. Anderson's Memoirs.* New York: New World, 1970.

Auerbach, Carl A. "Presidential Administration of Prices and Wages," *George Washington Law Review* 35 (December 1966): 191–251.

Ballard, Jack Stokes. "The Shock of Peace: Military and Economic Demobilization after World War II." Ph.D. dissertation, University of California, Los Angeles, 1974.

Bernstein, Barton J. "America in War and Peace," in *Towards a New Past: Dissenting Essays in American History.* New York: Pantheon, 1968.

————. "Clash of Interests: The Postwar Battle between the Office of Price Administration and the Department of Agriculture," *Agricultural History* 41 (January 1967): 45–57.

————. "Economic Policies," in *The Truman Period as a Research Field,* ed. Richard S. Kirkendall, pp. 87–148. Columbia: University of Missouri Press, 1967.

————. "The Postwar Famine and Price Control, 1946," *Agricultural History* 38 (October 1964): 235–40.

Blackman, John L., Jr. *Presidential Seizure in Labor Disputes.* Cambridge: Harvard University Press, 1967.

Blum, Albert A. "Mobilization of Men and Machines during the Second World War," in *World War II: An Account of its*

Documents, ed. James E. O'Neill and Robert W. Krauskopf, pp. 183–88. Washington, D.C.: Howard University Press, 1976.

Blum, John Morton. *From the Morgenthau Diaries: Years of War, 1941–1945.* Boston: Houghton Mifflin, 1967.

——————. *V Was for Victory: Politics and American Culture during World War II.* New York: Harcourt Brace Jovanovich, 1976.

——————. ed. *The Price of Vision: The Dairy of Henry A. Wallace, 1942–1946.* Boston: Houghton Mifflin, 1973.

Blyth, Conrad A. *American Business Cycles, 1945–1950.* New York: Praeger, 1969.

Bowles, Chester. *Promises to Keep: My Years in Public Life, 1941–1969.* New York: Harper & Row, 1971.

Boylan, James R. "Reconversion in Politics: The New Deal Coalition and the Election of the Eightieth Congress." Ph.D. dissertation, Columbia University, 1971.

Brady, Patrick George. "Toward Security: Postwar Economic and Social Planning in the Executive Office, 1939–1946." Ph.D. dissertation, Rutgers University, 1975.

Cady, Darrel. "The Truman Administration's Reconversion Policies, 1945–1947." Ph.D. dissertation, University of Kansas, 1974.

Cochran, Bert. *Harry S. Truman and the Crisis Presidency.* New York: Funk & Wagnalls, 1973.

Cochrane, Willard W., and Ryan, Mary E. *American Farm Policy, 1948–1973.* Minneapolis: University of Minnesota Press, 1976.

Copp, E. Anthony. *Regulating Competition in Oil: Government Intervention in the U.S. Refining Industry, 1948–1975.* College Station: Texas A & M University Press, 1976.

Cormier, Frank, and Eaton, William J. *Reuther.* Englewood Cliffs, N.J.: Prentice-Hall, 1970.

Craig, Richard B. *The Bracero Program: Interest Groups and Foreign Policy.* Austin: University of Texas Press, 1971.

Cypher, James M. "Military Expenditures and the Performance of the Postwar U.S. Economy: 1947–1971." Ph.D. dissertation, University of California, Riverside, 1973.

DiBacco, Thomas V. " 'Draft the Strikers (1946) and Seize the Mills (1952)': The Business Reaction," *Duquesne Review* 13, no. 2 (Fall 1968): 63–75.

Dobney, Fredrick J. "The Evolution of Reconversion Policy: World War II and Surplus War Property Disposal," *The Historian* 36 (May 1974): 498–519.

Dodds, Gordon B. "Conservation and Reclamation in the Trans-Mississippi West: A Critical Bibliography, *Arizona and the West* 13 (Summer 1971): 143–71.

Donovan, Robert J. *Conflict and Crisis: The Presidency of Harry S. Truman, 1945–1948.* New York: W. W. Norton, 1977.

Douglas, Paul H. *In the Fullness of Time: The Memoirs of Paul II. Douglas.* New York: Harcourt Brace Jovanovich, 1972.

Dubofsky, Melvyn, and Van Tine, Warren. *John L. Lewis: A Biography.* New York: Quadrangle Books, 1977.

Eccles, Marriner S. *Beckoning Frontiers: Public and Personal Recollections.* New York: Knopf, 1951.

Ferrell, John R. "Water in the Missouri: The Inter-Agency Concept at Mid-Century," *Journal of the West* 7 (January 1968): 96–105.

Ficken, Robert E. "The Democratic Party and Domestic Politics during World War II." Ph.D. dissertation, University of Washington, 1973.

Forsythe, James L. "Clinton P. Anderson: Politician and Businessman as Truman's Secretary of Agriculture." Ph.D. dissertation, University of New Mexico, 1970.

Foster, James Caldwell. *The Union Politic: The CIO Political Action Committee.* Columbia: University of Missouri Press, 1975.

Fusfeld, Daniel R. *The Economic Thought of Franklin D. Roosevelt and the Origins of the New Deal.* New York: Columbia University Press, 1956.

Garson, Robert A. "The Alienation of the South: A Crisis for Harry S. Truman, 1945–1948," *Missouri Historical Review* 64 (July 1970): 448–71.

——————. *The Democratic Party and the Politics of Sectionalism, 1941–1948.* Baton Rouge: Louisiana State University Press, 1974.

Goodwin, Crauford D., and Herren, R. Stanley. "The Truman Administration: Problems and Policies Unfold," in *Exhortation and Controls: The Search for a Wage-Price Policy,*

1945–1971, ed. Crauford D. Goodwin, pp. 9–93. Washington, D.C.: The Brookings Institution, 1975.

Goulden, Joseph C. *The Best Years, 1945–50.* New York: Atheneum, 1976.

Graham, Otis L., Jr. *Toward a Planned Society: From Roosevelt to Nixon.* New York: Oxford University Press, 1976.

Green, James. "Working Class History in the 1940s: A Bibliographical Essay," *Radical America* 9 (July-August 1975): 206–13.

Griffith, Robert. "Truman and the Historians: The Reconstruction of Postwar American History," *Wisconsin Magazine of History* 59 (Autumn 1975): 20–50.

Hairgrove, Kenneth D. "Sam Rayburn: Congressional Leader, 1940–1952." Ph.D. dissertation, Texas Tech University, 1974.

Hamby, Alonzo L. *Beyond the New Deal: Harry S. Truman and American Liberalism.* New York: Columbia University Press, 1973.

——————. "The Liberals, Truman, and FDR as Symbol and Myth," *Journal of American History* 56 (March 1970): 859–67.

——————. "Sixty Million Jobs and the People's Revolution: The Liberals, The New Deal, and World War II," *The Historian* 30 (August 1968): 578–98.

——————. "The Vital Center, the Fair Deal, and the Quest for a Liberal Political Economy," *American Historical Review* 77 (June 1972): 653–78.

Hand, Samuel B. *Counsel and Advice: A Political Biography of Samuel I. Rosenman.* New York: Garland, 1979.

Hartmann, Susan M. *Truman and the 80th Congress.* Columbia: University of Missouri Press, 1971.

Hasting, Ann Celest. "Intraparty Struggle: Harry S. Truman, 1945–1948." Ph.D. dissertation, St. Louis University, 1972.

Heath, Jim F. "Domestic America during World War II: Research Opportunities for Historians," *Journal of American History* 58 (September 1971): 384-414.

Herren, Robert Stanley. "Wage-Price Policy during the Truman Administration: A Postwar Problem and the Search for its Solution." Ph.D. dissertation, Duke University, 1975.

Howerton, Joseph. "The Record of Federal Emergency Civilian Control," in *World War II: An Account of its Documents,* ed. James E. O'Neill and Robert W. Krauskopf, pp. 189–210. Washington, D.C.: Howard University Press, 1976.

Huthmacher, J. Joseph. *Senator Robert F. Wagner and the Rise of Urban Liberalism.* New York: Atheneum, 1968.

Hyman, Sidney. *Marriner S. Eccles: Private Entrepreneur and Public Servant.* Stanford, Calif.: Stanford University Graduate School of Business, 1976.

Johnson, Arthur M. *Petroleum Pipelines and Public Policy, 1906–1959.* Cambridge: Harvard University Press, 1967.

Jones, Byrd. "The Role of Keynesians in Wartime Policy and Postwar Planning, 1940–1956," *American Economic Review* 62 (May 1972): 125–33.

Jones, E. Terrence. "Congressional Voting on Keyensian Legislation, 1945–1964," *Western Political Quarterly* 21 (June 1968): 240–51.

Kathka, David A. "The Bureau of Reclamation in the Truman Administration: Personnel, Politics, and Policy." Ph.D. dissertation, University of Missouri, 1976.

Kevles, Daniel J. "The National Science Foundation and the Debate over Postwar Research Policy, 1942–1945: A Political Interpretation of *Science—The Endless Frontier,*" *Isis* 68 (March 1977): 5–26.

Keyserling, Leon H. "The Council of Economic Advisers since 1946: Its Contributions and Failures," *Atlantic Economic Journal* 6 (March 1978): 17–35.

Kirkendall, Richard S. "Election of 1948," in *History of American Presidential Elections, 1789–1968,* ed. Arthur M. Schlesinger, Jr. and Fred L. Israel, 4: 3099–145. New York: Chelsea House, 1971.

——————. "Harry Truman," in *America's Eleven Greatest Presidents,* ed. Morten Borden, pp. 255–88. Chicago: Rand McNally, 1971.

——————, ed. *The Truman Period as a Research Field.* Columbia: University of Missouri Press, 1967.

——————, ed. *The Truman Period as a Research Field: A Reappraisal, 1972.* Columbia: University of Missouri Press, 1974.

Kirstein, Peter N. "Agribusiness, Labor, and the Wetbacks: Truman's Commission on Migratory Labor," *The Historian* 40 (August 1978): 650–67.

Koistinen, Paul A. C. "Mobilizing the World War II Economy:

Labor and the Industrial Military Alliance," *Pacific Historical Review* 42 (November 1973): 443–78.

Koppes, Clayton R. "Conservation and the Continuity of American Liberalism, 1933–1953." *California Institute of Technology Social Science Working Paper,* no. 174 (August 1977), pp. 1–46.

——————. "Oscar Chapman: A Liberal at the Interior Department, 1933–1953." Ph.D. dissertation, University of Kansas, 1974.

——————. "Public Water, Private Land: Origins of the Acreage Limitation Controversy, 1933–1953," *Pacific Historical Review* 47 (November 1978): 607–36.

Krooss, Herman. *Executive Opinion: What Business Leaders Said and Thought on Economic Issues, 1920s–1960s.* Garden City, N.Y.: Doubleday, 1970.

Lammie, Wayne D. "Unemployment in the Truman Administration: Political, Economic and Social Aspects." Ph.D. dissertation, Ohio State University, 1973.

Lee, Lawrence B. "100 Years of Reclamation Historiography," *Pacific Historical Review* 47 (November 1978): 507–64.

Lee, R. Alton. "The Truman–80th Congress Struggle over Tax Policy," *The Historian* 33 (November 1970): 68–82.

——————. *Truman and Taft-Hartley: A Question of Mandate.* Lexington: University of Kentucky Press, 1966.

Lichtenstein, Nelson N. "Industrial Unionism under the No-Strike Pledge: A Study of the CIO during the Second World War." Ph.D. dissertation, University of California, Berkeley, 1974.

Lomask, Milton. *A Minor Miracle: An Informal History of the National Science Foundation.* Washington, D.C.: G.P.O., 1976.

McClure, Arthur F. *The Truman Administration and the Problems of Postwar Labor, 1945–1948.* Rutherford, N.J.: Associated University Presses, 1969.

MacDonald, Robert M. "Collective Bargaining in the Postwar Period," *Industrial and Labor Relations Review* 20 (July 1967): 553–77.

Maddox, Robert F. "Senator Harley M. Kilgore and World War II." Ph.D. dissertation, University of Kentucky, 1974.

Marcus, Maeva. *Truman and the Steel Seizure Case: The Limits of Presidential Power.* New York: Columbia University Press, 1977.

Markowitz, Norman D. *The Rise and Fall of the People's Century: Henry A. Wallace and American Liberalism, 1941–1948.* New York: Free Press, 1973.

Matusow, Allen. *Farm Policies and Politics in the Truman Years.* Cambridge: Harvard University Press, 1967.

Meeker, Thomas A., comp. *The Military-Industrial Complex: A Source Guide to the Issues of Defense Spending and Control.* Los Angeles: California State University Center for the Study of Armament and Disarmament, 1973.

Mills, Daniel Quinn. *Government, Labor, and Inflation: Wage Stabilization in the United States.* Chicago: University of Chicago Press, 1975.

Morrison, Denton E., comp. *Energy: A Bibliography of Social Science and Related Literature.* New York: Garland, 1975.

Morrison, Denton E.; Hornback, Kenneth E.; and Warner, W. Keith, comps. *Environment: A Bibliography of Social Science and Related Literature.* Washington, D.C.: G.P.O., 1973.

Mrozek, Donald J. "The Truman Administration and the Enlistment of the Aviation Industry in Postwar Defense," *Business History Review* 48 (Spring 1974): 73–94.

Nagle, Richard W. "Collective Bargaining in Basic Steel and the Federal Government, 1945–1960." Ph.D. dissertation, Pennsylvania State University, 1978.

Nash, Gerald D. *United States Oil Policy, 1890–1964: Business and Government in Twentieth Century America.* Pittsburgh: University of Pittsburgh Press, 1968.

Neustadt, Richard E. *Presidential Power: The Politics of Leadership.* New York: John Wiley, 1960.

Norton, Hugh S. *The Employment Act and the Council of Economic Advisers, 1946–1976.* Columbia: University of South Carolina Press, 1977.

Olson, John M. D., Jr. "An Analysis of Fiscal Policy during the Truman Administration (1945–1953)." Ph.D. dissertation, University of South Carolina, 1966.

Partin, John W. " 'Assistant President' for the Home Front: James F. Byrnes and World War II." Ph.D. dissertation, University of Florida, 1977.

Patterson, James T. *Mr. Republican: A Biography of Robert A. Taft.* Boston: Houghton Mifflin, 1972.

Pemberton, William E. "Executive Reorganization during the Truman Administration, 1945 through 1950." Ph.D. dissertation, University of Missouri, 1975.

Perrett, Geoffrey. *Days of Sadness, Years of Triumph: The American People, 1939–1945.* New York: Coward, McCann and Geoghegan, 1973.

Peterson, F. Ross. *Prophet without Honor: Glen H. Taylor and the Fight for American Liberalism.* Lexington: University Press of Kentucky, 1974.

Peterson, Gale E. "President Harry S. Truman and the Independent Regulatory Commissions, 1945–1952." Ph.D. dissertation, University of Maryland, 1973.

Phillips, Cabell. *The Truman Presidency: The History of a Triumphant Succession.* New York: Macmillan, 1966.

Polenberg, Richard. "Historians and the Liberal Presidency: Recent Appraisals of Roosevelt and Truman," *South Atlantic Quarterly* 75 (Winter 1976): 20–35.

—————. *War and Society: The United States, 1941–1945.* Philadelphia: Lippincott, 1972.

Pursell, Carroll. "Alternative American Science Policies during World War II," in *World War II: An Account of Its Documents,* ed. James E. O'Neill and Robert W. Krauskopf, pp. 151–62. Washington, D.C.: Howard University Press, 1976.

Rasmussen, Wayne D., ed. *Agriculture in the United States: A Documentary History.* 4 vols. New York: Random House, 1975.

Reuther, Victor G. *The Brothers Reuther and the Story of the UAW.* Boston: Houghton Mifflin, 1976.

Richardson, Elmo R. *Dams, Parks & Politics: Resource Development & Preservation in the Truman-Eisenhower Era.* Lexington: University Press of Kentucky, 1973.

Rosenof, Theodore. "The Economic Ideas of Henry Wallace, 1933–1948," *Agricultural History* 41 (April 1967): 143–53.

Ross, Davis R. B. *Preparing for Ulysses: Politics and Veterans during World War II.* New York: Columbia University Press, 1969.

Ross, Irwin. *The Loneliest Campaign: The Truman Victory of 1948.* New York: New American Library, 1968.

Roukis, George S. "American Labor and the Conservative Republicans, 1946–1948: A Study in Economic and Political Conflict." Ph.D. dissertation, New York University, 1973.

Salant, Walter S. "Some Intellectual Contributions of the Truman Council of Economic Advisers to Policy-Making," *History of Political Economy* 5 (Spring 1973): 36–49.

Saloutos, Theodore. "Agricultural Organizations and Farm Policy in the South after World War II," *Agricultural History* 53 (January 1979): 377–404.

Sawyer, Charles. *Concerns of a Conservative Democrat.* Carbondale: Southern Illinois University Press, 1968.

Schaefer, Arthur M. "Presidential Intervention in Labor Disputes during the Truman Administration: A History and Analysis of Experience." Ph.D. dissertation, University of Pennsylvania, 1967.

Schapsmeier, Edward L., and Schapsmeier, Frederick H. "Farm Policy from FDR to Eisenhower: Southern Democrats and the Politics of Agriculture," *Agricultural History* 53 (January 1979): 352–71.

—————. *Prophet in Politics: Henry A. Wallace and the War Years, 1940–1965.* Ames: Iowa State University Press, 1970.

Schoenebaum, Eleanora, ed. *Political Profiles: The Truman Years.* New York: Facts on File, 1978.

Schriftgiesser, Karl. *Business and Public Policy: The Role of the Committee for Economic Development, 1942–1967.* Englewood Cliffs, N.J.: Prentice-Hall, 1967.

Sharp, Bert M. " 'Bring the Boys Home': Demobilization of the United States Armed Forces after World War II." Ph.D. dissertation, Michigan State University, 1977.

Shogan, Robert. "1948 Election," *American Heritage Magazine* 19 (June 1968): 22–31, 104–11.

Shurbet, Joanna Healey. "John L. Lewis: The Truman Years." Ph.D. dissertation, Texas Tech University, 1975.

Sitkoff, Harvard. "Years of the Locust: Interpretations of the Truman Presidency since 1965," in *The Truman Period as a Research Field: A Reappraisal, 1972,* ed. Richard S. Kirkendall, pp. 75–112. Columbia: University of Missouri Press, 1974.

Smith, Geoffrey S. " 'Harry, We Hardly Know You': Revisionism, Politics and Diplomacy, 1945–1954," *American Political Science Review* 70 (June 1976): 560–82.

Stanley, David T.; Mann, Dean E.; and Doig, Jameson W. *Men Who Govern: A Biographical Profile of Federal Political Executives.* Washington, D.C.: Brookings Institution, 1967.

Stebbins, Phillip E. "Truman and the Seizure of Steel: A Failure in Communications," *The Historian* 34 (November 1971): 1–21.

Stein, Herbert. *The Fiscal Revolution in America.* Chicago: University of Chicago Press, 1969.

Steinberg, Alfred. *Sam Rayburn: A Biography.* New York: Hawthorn, 1975.

Steinmeyer, George W. "Disposition of Surplus War Property: An Administrative History, 1944–1949." Ph.D. dissertation, University of Oklahoma, 1969.

Stoesen, Alexander R. "The Senatorial Career of Claude D. Pepper." Ph.D. dissertation, University of North Carolina, 1965.

Tavlas, George S. "The Chicago Tradition Revisited: Some Neglected Monetary Contributions, Senator Paul Douglas," *Journal of Money, Credit and Banking* 9 (November 1977): 529–35.

Templeton, Ronald K. "The Campaign of the American Federation of Labor and the Congress of Industrial Organizations to Prevent Passage of the Labor-Management Relations Act of 1947." Ph.D. dissertation, Ball State University, 1967.

Theoharis, Athan. "The Truman Presidency: Trial and Error," *Wisconsin Magazine of History* 55 (Autumn 1971): 49–58.

Vatter, Harold G. *The U.S. Economy in the 1950s: An Economic History.* New York: W. W. Norton, 1963.

Wagnon, William O., Jr. "John Roy Steelman: Native Son to Presidential Adviser" *Arkansas Historical Quarterly* 26 (Autumn 1968): 205–25.

—————. "The Politics of Economic Growth: The Truman Administration and the 1949 Recession." Ph.D. dissertation, University of Missouri, 1970.

Wallace, Harold. "The Campaign of 1948." Ph.D. dissertation, Indiana University, 1970.

Warken, Philip W. *A History of the National Resources Planning Board, 1933–1943.* New York: Garland, 1979.

Warne, William E. *The Bureau of Reclamation.* New York: Praeger, 1973.

Weidenbaum, Murray L. "The Need for Reframing the M-I Relationship," in *The Political Economy of the Military-*

Industrial Complex, ed. Warren F. Ilchman and Joe S. Bain, pp. 55–94. Berkeley: University of California Institute of Business and Economic Research, 1973.

Weintraub, R. E. "Some Neglected Monetary Contributions: Congressman Wright Patman (1893–1976)," *Journal of Money, Credit and Banking* 9 (November 1977): 517–28.

Whitnah, Donald R. *Safer Skyways: Federal Control of Aviation, 1926–1966.* Ames: Iowa State University Press, 1966.

Wiltz, John E. "The Korean War and American Society," in *The Korean War: A 25-Year Perspective,* ed. Francis H. Heller, pp. 112–58. Lawrence: Regents Press of Kansas.

Yarnell, Allen. *Democrats and Progressives: The 1948 Election as a Test of Postwar Liberalism.* Berkeley: University of California Press, 1974.

Some Primary Sources on Economics
And the Truman Administration

MANUSCRIPT COLLECTIONS

The figure in parenthesis indicates the number of linear feet of material in each collection at the Truman Library.

Adams, Russell B., member, Civil Aeronautics Board, 1948–50: Papers, 1944–53 (9)

Anderson, Clinton P., secretary of agriculture, 1945–48: Papers, 1945–48 (6)

Ball, Max W., director, Oil and Gas Division, Department of the Interior, 1947–48: Papers, 1944–54 (2)

Blaisdell, Thomas C., Jr., assistant secretary of commerce, 1949–51: Papers, 1933–51 (5)

Blough, Roy, member, Council of Economic Advisers, 1950–52: Papers, 1927–72 (19)

Chapman, Oscar L., secretary of the interior, 1949–53: Papers, 1931–53 (50)

Clark, John D., vice chairman, Council of Economic Advisers, 1950–53: Papers, 1946–52 (1)

Colm, Gerhard, assistant chief, Fiscal Division, Bureau of the Budget, 1940–46: Papers, 1944–47 (1)

Davidson, C. Girard, assistant secretary of the interior, 1946–50: Papers, 1940–50 (12)

Davies, Ralph K., deputy petroleum administrator for war, 1942–46: Papers, 1941–46 (9)

Dixon, William C., chief, Los Angeles Office, Anti-Trust Division, Department of Justice, 1948–54: Papers, 1944–54 (10)

Doty, Dale E., assistant secretary of the interior, 1950–52: Papers, 1939–54 (8)

Ecker-Racz, L. Laszlo, director, Tax Advisory Staff, Department of the Treasury, 1949–53: Papers, 1949–53 (3)

Edminster, Lynn R., vice chairman, U.S. Tariff Commission, 1942–53: Papers, 1925–69 (8)

Enarson, Harold L., special assistant in the White House Office, 1950–52: Papers, 1941–53 (3)

Foley, Raymond M., administrator, Housing and Home Finance Agency, 1947–53: Papers, 1946–53 (2)

Fox, Abijah U., deputy director, Finance Division, Military Government, Germany, 1946: Papers, 1941–46 (3)

Gibson, John W., assistant secretary of labor, 1946–50: Papers, 1935–54 (19)

Hennock, Frieda, member, Federal Communications Commission, 1948–55: Papers, 1948–55 (9)

Jones, J. Weldon, assistant director, Bureau of the Budget, 1941–55: Papers, 1929–72 (20)

Lawton, Frederick J., director, Bureau of the Budget, 1950–53: Papers, 1943–63 (5)

McCormick, Clarence J., undersecretary of agriculture, 1950–52: Papers, 1950–52 (1)

McGuire, Charles H., director, National Shipping Authority, 1951–53: Papers, 1951–55 (1)

Mehl, Joseph M., administrator, Commodity Exchange Authority, 1947–54: Papers, 1916–74 (14)

Murphy, Charles S., special counsel to the president, 1950–53: Papers, 1947–67 (18)

Pace, Frank, Jr., director, Bureau of the Budget, 1949–50: Papers, 1946–53 (7)

President's Advisory Committee on the Merchant Marine: Records, 1947 (7)

President's Air Policy Commission: Records, 1947–48 (16)

President's Commission on Migratory Labor: Records: 1950–51 (6)

President's Materials Policy Commission: Records, 1951–52 (55)

President's Water Resources Policy Commission: 1950–51 (25)

Rice, Stuart A., assistant director for statistical standards, Bureau of the Budget, 1940–55: Papers, 1900–69 (69)

Salant, Walter S., economist, Council of Economic Advisers, 1946–52: Papers, 1934–52 (1)

Snyder, John W., secretary of the treasury, 1946–53: Papers, 1918–71 (101)

Tenenbaum, Edward A., special assistant to the finance adviser, U.S. Military Government in Germany, 1945–48: Papers, 1941–59 (4)

Truman, Harry S., president of the United States, 1945–53: Papers, 1926–72 (2959)

Turner, Robert C., member, council of Economic Advisers, 1952–53: Papers, 1941–52 (2)

Webb, James E., director, Bureau of the Budget, 1946–49: Papers, 1928–75 (229)

Wolfsohn, Joel D., assistant secretary of the interior, 1952–53: Papers, 1926–61 (19)

ORAL HISTORY INTERVIEWS

The figure in parenthesis indicates the number of pages in each transcript at the Truman Library.

Baker, George P., director, Office of Transportation and Communications Policy, Department of State, 1945–46 (56)

Barnett, Robert W., economist, Department of State, 1945–54 (39)

Becker, Nathan M., economic adviser, General Staff, U.S.–UN Forces, Korea, 1952–53 (99)

Bohan, Merwin L., foreign service officer specializing in economic relations between the U.S. and Latin America, 1928–55 (84)

Cole, David L., director, Federal Mediation and Conciliation Service, 1952–53 (103)

Davidson, C. Girard, assistant secretary of the interior, 1946–50 (225)

Divers, William K., chairman, Home Loan Bank Board, 1947–54 (369)

Dux, Michael J., economist, Department of State, 1946–55 (49)

Eakens, Robert H. S., chief, Petroleum Policy Staff, Department of State, 1950–54 (55)

Ensley, Grover W., executive director, Joint Economic Committee, U.S. Congress, 1949–57 (91)

Gardner, Warner W., assistant secretary of the interior, 1946–47 (66)

Goldsmith, Raymond W., economist, Department of State, 1947–48 (39)

Jones, Roger W., assistant director, Bureau of the Budget, 1945–59 (126)

Keyserling, Leon H., vice chairman, 1946–50, and chairman, 1950–53, Council of Economic Advisers (208)

Kindleberger, Charles P., chief, Division of German and Austrian Economic Affairs, Department of State, 1945–48 (118)

Lawton, Frederick J., director, Bureau of the Budget, 1950–53 (71)

Leddy, John M., staff member, Trade Agreements Division, Department of State, 1945–58 (80)

McDiarmid, O. J., chief, Monetary Affairs Staff, Department of State, 1949–51 (51)

Maffry, August, vice president and economic adviser, Export-Import Bank, 1945–47 (38)

Newcomb, Robinson, economist, Council of Economic Advisers, 1947–50 (59)

Nourse, Edwin G., chairman, Council of Economic Advisers, 1947–49 (121)

Pace, Frank, Jr., director, Bureau of the Budget, 1949–50 (174)

Salant, Walter, economist, Council of Economic Advisers, 1946–52 (98)

Seidman, Harold D., staff member, Bureau of the Budget, 1943–68 (158)

Snyder, John W., secretary of the treasury, 1946–53 (1932)

Sundquist, James L., administrative analyst, Bureau of the Budget, 1941–47, 1949–51 (56)

Thorp, Willard L., assistant secretary of state for economic affairs, 1946–52 (182)

Vernon, Raymond, assistant director, International Resources Division, Department of State, 1946–48 (62)

Young, John P., chief, Division of International Finance, Department of State, 1943–65 (85)

Index